The Saskatchewan Secret:

Folk Healers, Diviners, and Mystics of the Prairies

Jacqueline Moore

benchmark

press

The author may be contacted at folkhealers@sasktel.net.

Grateful acknowledgement is made to Joni Mitchell and Alfred Publishing Co. for permission to reprint lines from "Woodstock," to Rena Jeanne Hanchuk and the Canadian Institute of Ukrainian Studies for permission to reprint excerpts from *The Word and Wax: A Medical Folk Ritual Among Ukrainians in Alberta*, and to Francesca Iosca-Pagnin for permission to reprint excerpts from *Reflections 'NPink*.

Lyrics from "Circle" copyright of Harry Chapin Foundation. Music and lyrics by Harry Chapin, harrychapinmusic.com. Used with permission. Not to be copied or reprinted.

Every effort has been made to trace copyright holders and to obtain their permission for the use of copyright material.

Kahlee Keane photo by Melissa Kelly. All other photos by Jacqueline Moore.

The author of this book does not dispense medical advice or prescribe the use of any technique as a form of treatment for physical, emotional, or spiritual problems. The intent of this book is only to offer information of a general nature.

The author gratefully acknowledges the assistance of the Saskatchewan Arts Board.

Printed and bound in Canada.

Text pages printed on 100% recycled paper.

Library and Archives Canada Cataloguing in Publication

Moore, Jacqueline, 1967-
The Saskatchewan secret : folk healers, diviners and
mystics of the Prairies / Jacqueline Moore.

ISBN 978-0-9813243-2-6

1. Traditional medicine--Saskatchewan.
2. Healers--Saskatchewan. I. Title.

GR880.M66 2009   615.8'809227124   C2009-905791-3

Mixed Sources
Cert no. SW-COC-001271
© 1996 FSC
FSC

ENVIRONMENTAL BENEFITS STATEMENT
Benchmark Press saved the following resources by printing the pages of this book on chlorine free paper made with 100% post-consumer waste.

TREES	WATER	SOLID WASTE	GREENHOUSE GASES
10	4,514	274	937
FULLY GROWN	GALLONS	POUNDS	POUNDS

Calculations based on research by Environmental Defense and the Paper Task Force
Manufactured at Friesens Corporation

Dedication

*For Scott: My best friend, my rock, and
the reason I believe in fairytales.*

Acknowledgements

This project came into being thanks to the Saskatchewan Arts Board. The validation from the board was an incredible incentive to this first-time author, and the two grants were greatly appreciated.

It was the Saskatchewan Writers' Guild (SWG) and their wonderful program officer Amy Nelson-Mile that helped the project become a book. Two of these stories won literary awards from the SWG, and one was published in their *spring* magazine. Further, you wouldn't be holding this book if it weren't for the mentorship of J. Jill Robinson and editing of David Carpenter, both facilitated by the SWG.

Thank you Jill, for helping shape these characters and anecdotes into real stories – and for shaping me into a narrator. Thank you David, for your insights and genuine enthusiasm which sparked new energy in the manuscript. I'm honoured to call you both my friends.

Throughout this, I've been extremely lucky to have such solid support and love from family and friends. I'm thankful to my mother Darien for her integrity, her belief in the magic, and her eagle-eye editing; and to my 'other mother' Rebecca for her encouragement and her fantastic ability to keep up the fun. I'm grateful to my amazing and beautiful long-time sisters: Jennifer, who features in one of these stories (and a million of my personal ones); Gillian, who felt and brought a profundity to this project; Evelyn for her sweet, steady belief in me. And I'm ever-thankful to my dear pal Greg who appears in two of these stories (and at all my major moments).

Special thanks to Warren Goulding, Kahlee Keane, Al O'Neil, Terren Turner, Jan Henrikson, Wanda Johnson, Chrissy Krowchenko, Karen Pidskalny, Rachel MacDonald, Gary Zyla, Happy Grove, Audrey Taylor, Tracy Sheppard, Sean Sass, Bill Klebeck, Isabel Huggan, Warren Cariou, Michael Trussler and Susan Musgrave.

Most of all, I'm indebted to the healers who shared so much of themselves for this book. To me, these 13 people embody the unique personality of this little-known part of the world. It's a straightforward practicality, an almost shy modesty, and a heartbreaking generosity. It's so blithely yet fiercely Saskatchewanian – and it makes me so damn proud to be one.

There once was a wise sage who wandered the countryside. One day, as he passed near a village, he was approached by a woman who saw he was a sage and told him of a sick child nearby. She beseeched him to help this child. The sage came to the village, and a crowd gathered around him, for such a man was a rare sight. One woman brought the sick child to him, and he said a prayer over her.

"Do you really think your prayer will help her, when medicine has failed?" yelled a man from the crowd.

"You know nothing of such things! You are a stupid fool!" said the sage to the man.

The man became very angry with these words and his face grew hot and red. He was about to say something, or perhaps strike out, when the sage walked over to him and said: "If one word has such power as to make you so angry and hot, may not another have the power to heal?"

And thus, the sage healed two people that day.

(author unknown)

Table of Contents

Preface

For many years now, I have been intrigued with stories of Saskatchewan folk medicine. I'm all ears when someone mentions an elderly healer at Whitefox who, with one treatment, relieved a farmer's 25-year limp. And I'm full of questions when I'm told of a terminally ill person being miraculously cured by "an old lady who lives by a lake near Debden – or was it Leoville?"

There is a fable-like quality to the stories. Often the anecdotes come from second or third-hand sources – as in "My aunt's friend went to see this healer …" – so the actual name of the healer or their whereabouts is vague. There is an elusiveness about these people, a mystique. Word-of-mouth is usually the only channel to learn of them, but it's an effective and age-old prairie method of separating the wheat from the chaff.

Their techniques for healing are highly individualistic. Some use local plants to treat illness, some heal by putting their hands on the injury, some pray, some find answers in a person's palm or on the soles of their feet, and some commune with spirits to receive their guidance.

Much as I wanted to head out and meet these amazing folks I'd been hearing of, I never had a legitimate reason to. I had no obvious illness and I didn't want to waste their valuable time with my idle curiosity. However in 2005, thanks to a grant from the Saskatchewan Arts Board, I found myself with some financial support and a bona fide mission: to acknowledge some of our unsung folk healers by writing their stories. I set out to experience who they were and where they lived; I wanted to find out when it was that they realized they could heal, how that has affected their life, and what they have learned along the way.

In Saskatchewan, there is a strong history of folk medicine. Especially in rural areas, many communities relied on their local healers for generations when university-trained doctors were simply not available. Often these practitioners were of a certain heritage and had been mentored in cultural healing techniques by their elders; First Nations, Métis, Ukrainian and

Mennonite* traditions all have distinct healing rituals.

I had determined several criteria for choosing which people I would interview. Paramount was that they would have no formal schooling in the healing arts. I wanted to talk to people whose healing abilities were innate or passed down in their families. Another condition was that they didn't advertise their services; as much as possible, I wanted to find healers who weren't making a commercial business out of their craft. In keeping with that, I looked for people who didn't charge specific fees for their treatments. (Within this book, there are a couple of cases where not every criterion was met, but these people very much warranted inclusion.) As well, I preferred the healer's name to come to me through someone they had helped, a personal reference. Lastly, I sought out people who did not make claims that they could cure illness. (This appealed to my own sensibilities; I was looking for a quiet humility as opposed to an extroverted charisma.)

The folk healers I spoke to were often born with a gift for 'seeing' or 'feeling.' Most of them told me they tried in vain to suppress this in their younger years. It seems their gift chose them, rather than them choosing to heal.

I kept an open mind during the process of seeking out and connecting with these various people. At times though, I admit I felt some trepidation. In venturing out alone to meet unusual people who are sensitive enough to feel energy, to see pathologies within the body, to hear spirits . . . well, I wasn't sure what to expect.

What I found was openness and sincerity. Each of these healers was welcoming and truly interested in helping other people. Moreover, I was impressed by their humbleness; none of these people took personal credit for healing, and all attributed any success to their concept of the Divine.

Many times I felt we were in sacred space when the healers shared their stories or provided treatment. There were certain moments I even caught glimpses into different dimensions, moments that were inexplicable in normal reality.

I am deeply thankful to each of these people for inviting me into their homes and being so trusting and giving. All 13 of these individuals made a profound impact on me.

This book chronicles one person's experience of meeting only a handful of Saskatchewan's folk healers. There are many knowledgeable and respected healers in this province, but these are the particular ones that came my way. For that, I am honoured and grateful.

Jacqueline Moore
Saskatoon, 2009

The Mennonites have a fascinating history of healing; unfortunately their particular tradition seems to be dying with their elders. Around Saskatoon, there are several strong Mennonite communities and I was given the names of half a dozen one-time bonesetters. Sadly, most of them had already passed on and I wasn't able to find enough data to compile a story. 'Bonesetters' or 'trachmackja' were probably most comparable to present-day chiropractors. They were able to set all manner of fractures and broken bones, and treat sprains and dislocations – both in people and in livestock. The bonesetters, women and men, tended to be the community midwives as well. Most of them could not explain their gift and viewed it as something from God. My thanks to Leonard Doell of Aberdeen for providing me with local research and names, and to Sarah Reddekopp of Warman for sharing with me her personal stories of having been a bonesetter.

Author's Note

I need to say this upfront: I am not a skeptic. I'd say I keep fairly open-minded on matters of metaphysics and religion and the paranormal, all those heated topics that invite rigorous criticism. But that's not to say I have a cupboard full of snake oils.

Even more than not being a skeptic, I am not a dupe. In fact, I would describe myself as ultra-discerning and hyper-vigilant with others, often to a fault. Having grown up more independently than most, these are traits borne of necessity and honed with a lot of life experience. I've lived in big cities and small towns, had innumerable bizarre jobs, been in many unusual living arrangements, traveled off the beaten track around the world and met all kinds of extraordinary people ... and what got me through safely (besides sheer luck) was that I'm a good judge of character. Although I've lived an unorthodox life, it was always with an undercurrent of watchfulness and caution. And I long ago learned to steer clear of inauthentic people.

My belief system is based solidly on my life experience, but I'm well aware I haven't experienced everything. For instance, I'm not religious myself, but I respect absolutely other people's convictions about their particular god and gospel. Just because I haven't been led to those beliefs thus far doesn't mean I discount their legitimacy. Someone else's spiritual knowledge may not resonate within my own reality, but I appreciate that it does in theirs.

You know, 'reality' is a curious word – it sounds undeniable, authoritative, scientific. But it's a completely subjective concept. The fact is, four witnesses at the scene of a car accident will describe four separate scenarios; their answers will vary regarding seemingly indisputable facts like clothing description, time of day, what took place. Or four guests at the same dinner party will recount that evening differently because they each have their own unique perception: one will focus on the food more, while another will be more aware of the interplay between the guests. These individuals are truthfully depicting their version of reality; however, one's personal version must not be – *can not be* – the whole, entire and complete reality if three others are truthfully depicting differing versions.

Having long been aware that my own perceptions (and therefore, reality) are only one sliver of the complete pie, I am always interested in exploring other people's human experience – as long as I feel the person is genuine and has integrity.

While working on this project, I told a lot of friends and family about what I was doing and who I was interviewing, and I shared with them some of the healing anecdotes contained herein. I found that this particular subject is fascinating to many, but can become difficult when it challenges closely-held views on reality, God, the afterlife. I saw how even open-minded people would become defensive when they'd reached their personal boundaries of belief. On the other hand, the subject also inspired unexpected connections to strangers and many enlightening conversations; unsolicited, I was given a wealth of more information.

Dear reader, I suggest that you consider this book to be just that: information. It's not a dogma, it's not a sales pitch, it's not a testimonial. It is merely information which may be pertinent, or not, to you. In these pages, you'll be introduced to some unique and talented folks who have been gracious enough to share what they know. You need not alter your own knowledge and beliefs – whatever you believe is exactly right for you. I would ask that you simply accept that these are other good people's real experiences; and that you keep an open mind.

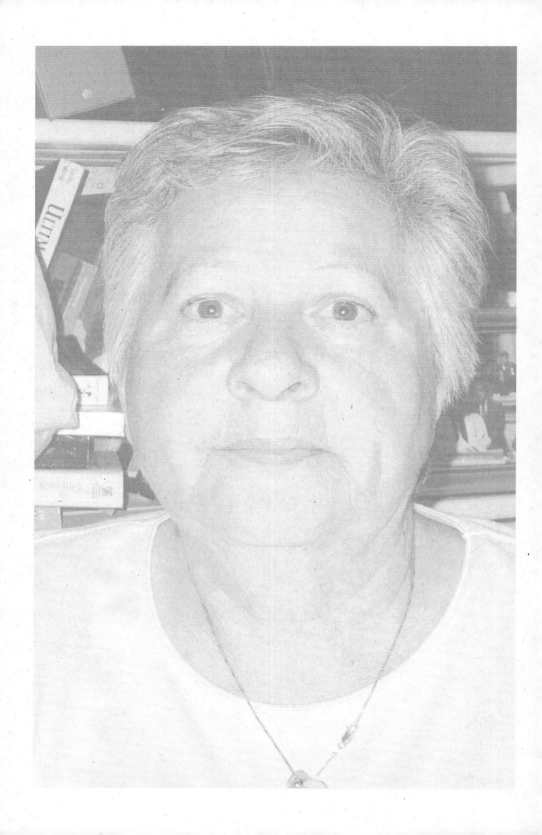

READING BETWEEN THE LINES

"The lines are not written into the human hands without reason, they come from heavenly influences and man's own individuality."

From *De coelo et mundi causa,* Aristotle

T he temperature is torrid in the low 30's on this August day – not a wisp of wind or cloud to cool it off. I'm making the 200-kilometre drive from Saskatoon to Moose Jaw. *'Goin' to see a woman about a palm,'* I quip to myself, then immediately shake my head. *Why must I always do a take on that old 'going to see a man about a dog' phrase – I don't even know where it's from!* I sigh. *I guess it's inane mind-chatter to exorcise anxious energy.* I guess I'm a little nervous.

I once visited a Chinese palm-reader on rue St. Denis in Montreal. Walking in, my companion and I thought it was just some entertainment. Instead, this man stated all sorts of personal truths about us, including very particular ones that no one could have guessed. The experience stunned me. I have since been more reverent toward the mysterious science of hand analysis. And in one hour from now, my past, my future, my weaknesses, my potential – and most unnerving to me, my life expectancy – will all be revealed to Betty McKenna, who is famous around these parts for her uncannily accurate palm-readings.

Passing Davidson, I ponder how an open hand can provide such a detailed personal map. Palmists study the three major lines on the palms – the Life Line, the Head Line and the Heart Line – as well as myriad secondary lines to determine one's personality, health, relationships, career, and spirituality. They also find information in the colour and texture of the skin, and the shape and length of the fingers and nails.

Certainly the practice of reading hands has been around for thousands of years; information on the principles of palmistry has been found in Vedic scripts, the Bible and early Semitic writings. According to Nathaniel Altman, palmistry researcher and author of six books on the subject, hand analysis is losing its association with gypsy fortune-telling, and is now being formally studied. He writes: *"Scientists at a number of major research centers, like the Galton Laboratory at University College in London and Emory University School of Medicine in Atlanta, have investigated the medical and psychological meanings of the lines and skin ridge patterns of the hand (known as dermatoglyphics), and a growing number of articles have been published about the . . . significance of hand analysis in reputable peer-reviewed journals like The American Journal of Cardiology, Nature and Gastroenterology."*

At the town of Chamberlain I turn right onto the pretty little #2 highway . . . getting closer! I'm excited about meeting Betty McKenna, too; I didn't think I'd get the opportunity. I had called her several times expressing my interest in interviewing her for this book, but she was too busy to meet with me. Betty is the full-time Elder-in-Residence for the Moose Jaw public school system. As well, she conducts regular work-shops on the seven teachings of her culture, the Anishnabe nation. A quick search on the internet also found her telling traditional stories for the Saskatchewan Library Association, storytelling at this year's Saskatchewan Showcase of the Arts conference, and sitting on the Builders Committee for the Moose Jaw Cultural Centre. However, months after my last request she phoned me, and in her light youthful voice, graciously offered to see me at 1:00 today, between her morning Summer Games volunteer shift, and her afternoon education meeting.

Now driving down into the valley where the Qu-Appelle River meets Buffalo Pound Lake, I recall my friend Joan's experience ten years ago when Betty read her palm. Betty told her she was a driven and ambitious person (no dispute there), that her father was an alcoholic (unfortunately true), and then she pointed out to Joan that there was a certain word inscribed in her palm, clear as day: it was 'tax.' Well, Joan had just gone through an emotional divorce and received a few thousand dollars in the settlement. It was income tax season, but she hadn't declared that money as she resented the government profiting over her failed marriage. However, with this word now imbedded in her hand, she felt that her guilt was clearly giving her away; once she left Betty's house, she immediately phoned her accountant to declare that extra income.

"And within a week or two, the word on my palm was gone," Joan told me, wide-eyed. "I could never find it there again."

According to hand analysts, the lines of the hand actually reflect our thinking, and as our attitudes and behaviour patterns change, the lines will physically change as well. *Just as a pebble thrown into the water creates ripples, so our thoughts create similar effects on our palms,"* wrote Michael Scotts in 1477, in one of the first books on palmistry ever penned.

Years after Joan's incident, I mentioned Betty to my friend Greg. He was intrigued so he, too, went to see her to get his palm read. "She told me several things about my health, like the fact that I was dehydrated, which I'd been told before by chiropractors," he said. "She told me 1972 was a significant year, and she was right – for some reason 1972 has always stuck with me. I remember my dad made a Christmas film of the family that year and in it, I'm holding up a piece of cardboard with '1972' written on it . . . I think of that year a lot," he added with a shrug. Betty had also informed Greg he would be well off in his 50s due to some shrewd investing (certainly Greg is on track for that, and intends to retire comfortably by then.) She told him he would be engaged but would not marry, and that he would have a long and happy relationship afterwards. This has all turned out to be true.

"And she said that, in six years, a very good friend would die at a young age of cancer," said Greg. "I asked her if that could already have happened and she said 'yes'." (This struck a chord. Greg was in the process of setting up a charitable foundation in the name of his dear friend who died, at 41, of cancer. She had died six years previously.)

It is precisely *that* ability in palmistry – to see death – that shakes me up. One time, Betty was asked what she does when she sees in a person's hand that they will die soon. She answered that it had happened twice: both times she feigned a headache and cancelled the session, and both times the person died within weeks.

Now watching for 'Hochelaga' on the Moose Jaw street signs, I find myself fretting. *If she has a headache today, I swear I'll have a heart attack on the spot . . . .*

I pull up and park in front of a modest home, in an older area of the city. I approach the side of the house and knock on the door. It opens, and a petite woman quietly invites me in. I enter a small crowded office space, with a window looking out to the front street, and on the opposite wall, a closed door leading to the rest of the house. After the searing sunlight, it takes a moment before my pupils recover to see the details: a computer on a long desktop, several shelves labouring under many stacks of books and papers, bulletin boards bustling with upcoming events and lists.

She motions for me to take an office chair, then seats herself three feet away from me in the other one. Betty is a diminutive woman, probably in her late 50s. Short, graying hair frames a surprisingly smooth and youthful face. She sits quietly, very upright, with her hands politely folded in her lap. She tends to gaze somewhere beyond my right temple rather than directly into my eyes. As an ice-breaker, I ask her about the bear claw hanging on her neck chain, and she tells me she is of the Bear Clan. She does not make small talk, though; she waits for me to ask questions, to initiate this session I've requested.

A reading normally takes about an hour and I know she has limited time for me today, but I just have a couple questions first . . . (*am I stalling?*) I start by asking her if it's 'palmistry' or 'hand analysis' that she does.

"I'll call it anything because I'm not too sure what it really is," says Betty. "I use the person's palm, but a lot of times the minute a person walks in the door I'm already picking up things. So I have no idea what it really is."

"And how long have you been doing it?" I ask.

"Oh, I'd have to say a person is born with the ability to do it, it isn't something that you learn," she says.

"Did you have a mentor, though? Someone to show you?"

"My grandmothers," says Betty. "They had that intuition, that's what I call it."

"So is palm-reading common in First Nations culture?" I wonder.

"For healing, for certain things, it is," she says. "Take a look at old Catlin drawings – some of those paintings he's done of people – and when they have a blue hand painted over the mouth, it indicates that they do what I do. Sometimes it's over the mouth, sometimes it's over the eye, showing that the person is a visionary, they can see into the future."

I ask if it's the same system for reading the palm that the Chinese or East Indians use.

"No," says Betty. "Because they write books on it, and I certainly couldn't write a book about it. When I look at your hand, I actually see the pictures – how do you put that in a book? Sometimes I can't make sense of what I'm seeing. I just tell you what it looks like to me, but I can't identify it."

"So do you get images simply by looking at people?"

"I see images sometimes, usually imbedded in the aura," she says, half in thought. Her head is tilted, she's studying a larger space around me. "A person can have four different colours surrounding them, and in those bands of colour, certain things appear that correspond to certain things that you are, that make up you. Those things being spiritual, mental, emotional and physical aspects."

I know this is cutting into my palm-reading session, but I'm curious. "Betty, what are the colours?"

"Yellow," she says without hesitation, "the first colour anybody has is yellow. And there are various colours of yellow. But all the other colours can change, through different emotions. There's also movement and sound. We're like a motor; every human being has a sound that is different from the others, so you can get a whole bunch of sounds in a room."

"Even if no one's speaking?"

"Yes," says Betty. "You also have light; that aura can be so vibrant that it's like four different coloured lights. And they have movements, they move different ways – some swirl around, some shoot out. The outermost aura that always sticks out can range from almost a clear colour to white – bright, brilliant white. It's our spiritual centre and that is the one that reaches out into the cosmos. I often see it with its lines and fingers going so far away you don't know where they're going, but they're connected to other people. I always just call them 'stringers.' Everybody has a stringer to something."

I'm reminded of something I read a few months ago, about a young healer from B.C. named Adam. As a small boy, Adam was already seeing auras, or what he calls "visual life energy," around every living thing; person, animal and plant. He says he found it overwhelming to go to a crowded mall or walk down the halls of his school because the multitude of auras was blindingly bright and overly distracting. By high school, he had learned to mute those energy fields so as to function more comfortably, but that information is still always accessible to him. As extensions of the physical body, Adam explains, the aura reflects problems in specific areas with different colours and a disruption of flow and movement.

"Can you *always* see people's auras?" I ask Betty.

"Always, yes," she answers, matter-of-factly.

"Do you have to turn that ability off sometimes, or do you use it in everyday life?"

"It's just always there," shrugs Betty. "I thought everybody had it, until I hit a certain age and told the wrong people and it really had some negative effect on me when I was a teenager. The way I describe it now though, is that when you go into a room and you see people, you know they have a nose. But you're not going to be analyzing a person's nose and staring at it. And you know they have ears, and you know they have a mouth, and you know they have an aura – all of it's just there, it's just a part of that person."

"But what you see in their auras must affect the way you perceive them," I say.

She nods.

"So how do you use that extra information in your life?"

"Well, there's a lot of people that are 'fakey'," says Betty. "Their aura says one thing about them, and they project something else (she puts her hands up as a block, to illustrate her reaction to them). So I say, 'Don't bother me, don't have anything to do with me, go be fake with somebody else!'"

We laugh. Yeah, I've met a few 'fakey' people myself along the way. But I remember that our time together is dwindling. "Betty, are there any specific palm readings you've done over the years that were especially clear or accurate?"

Betty thinks about that and says, "I can't say there are any that I've done that were *not* clear and accurate. Over the years people have come back to me, and verified the things that I had said to them. And it happened the way I said it would."

She says, for instance, some people would suddenly move when they'd had no previous intention of moving. "I'd say, 'You're getting a new job and you're moving,' and they'd say, 'No, I like my job and I like the place I'm living.' And within three weeks, the whole thing changes, they get promoted or something, and they move. One moved right from Saskatchewan to Ottawa."

Other times she described the business ventures they would be getting into, described the partner they would become involved with, described the person that would soon be interviewing them for a new job – and these things all happened.

"I can remember this one particular woman," says Betty. "I read her hand, and at the time she had five children – I told her she was going to have six." Betty smiles. "And she laughed and said, 'Well, that's impossible, there's no way I can, I've had my tubes tied.' But soon after, she got pregnant and she had the sixth child! Turns out what had happened was she was allergic to the plastic clips they used in the surgery, so she'd gone in and the doctor had removed them. She had also just gotten back together with her husband but," Betty chuckles, "before he went and got anything done, she was pregnant already! And she had a little boy – I see him walking around town."

I'm thinking what valuable insight this is to have, what an amazing resource Betty must be for her loved ones. "Do you read palms for your family?" I ask her.

"No, I never have." She is adamant. "You're not allowed to do it with your family."

I'm confused by this statement.

"Because if you do," she explains, "you could become controlling. When things aren't going the way you see it, you might try to manipulate your family. And you cannot do that. I don't do it with family."

We sit in silence for a moment. I find myself casting about for some provisional padding, a safety net to put in place before she looks at my palm. "Um, Betty, what I'm wondering is, can you *change* your destiny? Can you change what's in the palm if you change your actions?"

"My belief," says Betty, "is that when you come into this world, you've already made a contract with the Creator and you're at point A, and point B is when you go back to the Creator. So in the meantime, you have this 80 years maybe – some people have 40, some people have 20 – but you have the ability to take this journey and decide what you're going to do along the way. Which paths you will take, who you will talk to … if you look at it as a journey, as an undertaking, you are able to design the scenery for yourself. But the end result is that you're always going to get to point B."

I'm not convinced. In my lifetime, I've failed to deliver on some obligations; certainly I've missed a few deadlines. "But Betty," I venture, "what if you *don't* manage to fulfill your contract with the Creator?"

"Well I think you always fulfill the contract," she says. "I don't believe there's anybody that doesn't." Her voice softens now; she is barely audible. "I've sat with a lot of dying people as they leave this reality … and I believe when people get close to that, they know it and they make peace with themselves. That is part and parcel of stepping beyond, being back with the Creator. And then, I believe that the Creator just sends you back here, when you decide you need to do it again."

But what if somebody dies suddenly, like in a car accident, I ask her. Do they still have time to make peace?

"No," she says slowly. Thoughtfully.

I sense we are now on sacred territory, and I strain to hear her even though she's only three feet away. "If they die suddenly we always sing spirit – at least with the people that I was taught by. There's an Elder, Mary Louis, I work with from B.C. and we do 'cleaning.' We clean up where a spirit has departed quite suddenly, because the spirit is … shattered. And we sing it back into shape. You can feel it when they leave, when it's gathered back together. The families will ask me to go in and clean the place, to put the spirit back together."

Well, there's no turning back now. We are into it: the subject of death. The heat is stifling, I'm feeling fidgety – my aura is surely awhirl. "Betty, what do you do when you see terminal disease, or death, in a palm?"

"You want me to tell you the truth, I see death in everyone's hand. Because we're all going to die, no mistaking." She laughs lightly. "But in a person's hand, their Life Line will tell you how soon it might be. A lot of people ask about it, and I don't know *why* that fear of death is there, it's beyond my concept," she says, shaking her head. "It's limiting. We came from somewhere glorious, and we'll go back to it."

Oh, sweet soothing words. *Okay,* I think, *let's do it!* With only a half-hour left, I ask Betty if she would read my palm.

She affably agrees, and sets up a well-used TV tray between us, then methodically covers it with white sheets of paper. She brings out a large, hand-held magnifying glass. First she asks to look at the tops of my hands, so I suspend them above the white paper. She promptly tells me I am deficient in vitamin C and vitamin D. She says my thyroid needs a little attention. (Hmm, recent blood tests *did* show it was sluggish).

And then she spots it: the genetic weakness that plagued my paternal grandmother and killed my father at the age of 45. There is no alarm in her voice though, so in fact, I feel totally calm as it is said out loud. "I see heart disease in your gene pool," she states, dispassionately.

"Now turn your hands over, palms up," she says. I study her face as she gets her first glimpse of my Life Line: no reaction. "One hand you're born with and the other hand you make," she says. "One hand comes from the Creator, the other hand is where you can change things around, create your own scenery for the journey. The one closest to your heart is the one you're born with."

She shows me the faint Life Line I was born with, and how the Life Line I've created on my right hand is strong and deep and long. She says I've overcome some unfavourable genetic heredity, and will continue to do so. "The Life Line runs into the Mental Line, so it's your mental ability and your mental strength you'll use to do this for yourself." Mercifully, she is showing no sign of headache.

Looking at my hand through her magnifying glass, she says, "The other thing I can see is that your Spiritual Line right here," she says, pointing to my thumb, "is well connected. And that's one of the most fortunate lines to see well-marked."

She bends forward and cocks her head as she studies my hand through the glass. "There's this house in the country with lots of land, lots of green trees and water," she says. "There are three other people – I'm just telling you what I see because I see the pictures – and you're going there. It looks to me like everybody has a stake in that house, maybe it's a retreat house where other people come to get some healing. And these three people and you, so there'd be four people, would be doing different things to make this work." (I am silent. My husband and I have spent much of this summer building a large cabin for retreat – in 80 acres of secluded woods, surrounded by lots of green trees and water.)

Holding the magnifying glass in one hand, Betty is writing on the white paper with the other. She jots down several numbers which she says are significant to me, and then several dates; I ask her about the dates.

"There's something very special that occurs. All I know is I can see you really happy on these calendar dates. And these dates can be in different years." She reminds me that she sees images, but does not know whether they are past or future.

"I see a grey horse." (Interesting, because I've desperately wanted a horse since I was about three, and I'm thinking about it more these days as it's getting to be a possibility in my life. Greys, however, have never appealed to me – that is, until I saw 'Arctic Ice' this summer at the racetrack. A stately grey thoroughbred with black mane and tail, she was the most exquisite creature I'd ever seen. I bet on her that day, and later I dreamt of her. Now I watch for the greys.)

"And I see a dog, looks like some sort of a water dog." (Yes, we've agreed our next dog will be a Newfoundland retriever, especially because they love to swim.)

Betty sits up to look at the clock. Our time is pretty much up. I ask her if there's more still to see within my palm, if I should come visit her again to get the rest of the reading. In koan-like prose, she replies: "As you live life, things show on your hand. Sometimes as you live it, things that are muddy now become clearer. Anything else that I would take out of this, that hopefully a person would learn, is that life is good."

* * *

Driving home: past canola fields so yellow they make me weep, into skies so vast and humbling, I say 'thank you' aloud … I agree, life is good.

And Betty had told me I'll have plenty of time to enjoy it. She said I would live to be 93. I said that seemed impossible, I'd started smoking at age 11 and kept it up for 25 years, had done way more than my share of other health-damaging things along the way . . . and then there were the genes. She repeated it, with conviction. "Your palm indicates you will live to be 93 years old."

With that, she had declawed the silent, stalking fear I have always had of dying. Dying prematurely, that is.

"People come to me because they have some dis-ease about themselves," Betty had explained. "They're not comfortable with something, or they're anxious, or they have some healing to do and they need direction in that. That's why people come and I always figure the Creator sent them. So my whole goal in doing this is to help people realize something about themselves. It's to open the door to the possibilities that they may not have seen. Because a person never really looks at their true potential, they only look at their past experiences."

Yes. In my case, experiences that didn't foreshadow a lengthy life.

As I had been packing my notes and tape recorder to leave, I had remembered I wanted to take a photo of her. I took several pictures with the digital camera, and then held up the viewing screen to review them for her. Unintentionally, I went back an extra frame – to a picture I had taken last weekend of our cabin up north in the woods. I turned to her and said, "By the way, Betty, that's our house in the country."

Betty's face lit up and she exclaimed, "That *is* the house in the country! That's just what I saw!" We both laughed, giddy with this moment of proof.

And as I left, we performed an everyday gesture, developed centuries ago to show others that we are unarmed, and our intentions pure: we shook hands.

An open hand, it would seem, harbours no lies.

THE WAX POURER

Ceromancy: Divination by dropping melted wax in water

S he said I'd know I had the right place if there was a white house, a red
barn and a junky yard. Idling up the long gravel driveway, past a row
of old International trucks and silver silos, I'd say rather that this is a yard
full of history and life. There are chickens and horses grazing, unfenced,
amidst the farm machinery and assorted parts. A yellow kitten is calmly
giving itself a thorough cleaning not a foot away from the squirming,
tail-wagging blue heeler. Some bees buzz around the stacked white
compartments of their hive, while others are busy doing bee-things in the
various gardens. Several weathered wooden outbuildings stand in
community with the newer red barn, and beyond that, lush pastures wave
on the hills. Frankly, on this misty June morning, I'd even call this place
idyllic.

I had contacted Pauline Hnatiw of Bruno because she is one of the few
people in Saskatchewan still practicing an old Ukrainian tradition called
'wax-pouring.' The ceremony involves hot wax dropped into cold water,
prayers whispered over the water, and the hoped-for cure of all manner of
maladies in the patient. There is also a divining component, in which the
pourer can read in the wax certain qualities of their patients, and warn
them of potential hazards.

Rena Jeanne Hanchuk is the author of *The Word and Wax*, a book
about medical folk rituals among Ukrainians in Alberta. She writes: *"The*

wax ceremony was important at the time of immigration and in the years that immediately followed. It nullified fear, nervousness, sleeplessness, and restlessness, social and psychological disorders that occurred among people who had emigrated to a strange and foreign land. The ceremony was a culturally meaningful method of reducing stress and anxiety. The healers externalized these afflictions with their treatments and restored a sense of normality in their patients."

That's all I know about the tradition, and I have no idea what to expect from this meeting. But having no expectations is a good thing, I frequently find. It is then that I'm genuinely open to the entire experience.

I park along the verge and walk over to Pauline. In an old winter coat, she's hauling buckets of grain to a low, windowed chicken coop, handmade with this and that. She is in her late 60s, big-boned and dark-skinned – maybe from working outside for so many years. Her body teeters slightly, from left foot to right foot, as she walks. With no introduction, she says, "Want to see something beautiful? Come look at this!" She opens the coop hatch and makes some sweet 'shoorsh shoorsh' noises. Then several dozen fuzzy blonde baby geese come running out on gangly legs, flapping their stubby wings. She chuckles as they crowd toward her, chirping in great earnest. Pauline feeds the chicks and gives them fresh water, all the while speaking to them. "I talk to my animals," she explains. "I talk all the time and they talk back to me."

She recounts to me an incident when she was a young girl and five calves were stolen from the barn, and about another strange day when all the ducks had disappeared. Both times, Pauline says, she went outside at night when the air was clear and still, and called for the creatures. The calves, hearing her familiar voice, set to loudly bawling and thus were located in a shifty neighbour's barn. And the ducks, after some time, could be heard across a nearby field, making their noisy way home in response to her call. She laughs at the memory.

Pauline leads me over to an old horse trailer to show me this spring's ducklings inside under a heat lamp, and tells me about the Canada geese she raised six years ago when their mother was shot, and how one female has returned every year to nest on the shed. And then I follow her to the house.

Shoes off in the porch, we're now barefoot on the linoleum floor in the kitchen. An old black Labrador retriever trots in from the living room to bark at the stranger in his house; Pauline tells him to go lie down, and I watch him wander back and flomp down beside a long worktable presently occupied by a sewing machine and stacks of mending.

The kitchen is small and sparsely decorated, but comfortable. There is an Organic Crop Improvement Association certificate framed on a wall, and a Last Supper print above the table with a No Smoking sign tucked into the frame's edge. The wood cupboards look like they've seen many coats of white paint over the years. "I need to get the Hutterite girls in here to do a good cleaning," says Pauline, then marvels at how thorough and fast they are. "I have them in a few times a year, two of them will come and clean this whole house top to bottom – all the windows, the curtains, the cupboards – and by 4 o'clock they're done, and watching TV!" She says that TV is a real treat for them, and she likes the girls to be able to have some fun while they're at her house.

There's a sardine can on the floor, freshly licked out by the two pampered indoor cats. And there's a restaurant-style hot chocolate dispenser sitting on the counter, which we make good use of over the next few hours.

* * *

Pauline is immediately inclusive, telling me all sorts of frank and personal stories, unhindered by the newness of our acquaintance. Within no time, it feels like I'm a family member getting filled in on the latest goings-on after having been away for a few months. She speaks quickly – there's a lot of information and many anecdotes tumbling out.

I notice a dynamic yin-yang element to Pauline. Her voice is raspy, yet gentle and soothing. She is a beauty with thick hair, smooth skin and lovely bone structure, yet she has an undeniable toughness like a tomboy.

Her list of daily chores and projects is exhausting and relentless, yet she has an easygoing 'stay and visit' attitude. She lives in a very modest, somewhat austere house, but on several occasions says that she feels like the luckiest woman on earth. And although she never had a mother herself, she is caring and affectionate in a most maternal way.

She starts a lot of sentences with "My dear . . .," and many bits of advice are tucked into her stories: always feed the animals in the morning before you feed yourself – the animals are waiting and they depend on you; don't ever get so drunk you can't remember anything – that's when evil gets into your mind; don't drink cold water after heavy exertion – your lungs and stomach can seize right up so that you can't breathe in or out; always pray the moment you open your eyes in the morning, and just before you close your eyes in bed at night.

Pauline Hnatiw has known some potholes on the rocky road of life. An only child, she was rejected by her parents and raised by reluctant relatives. Married at 17, she spent some bleak years living with a demanding mother-in-law, followed by some hard times raising seven children on little money. She's been running the farm since her husband John became disabled with chronic health problems 25 years ago from working with farm chemicals (since then, their farm has been organic). Throughout it all, Pauline kept things going: she was a cook in northern camps, she drove a semi-trailer truck when farming income was lean, and she owned and ran two restaurants in nearby Humboldt by herself (thus the remnant hot chocolate dispenser). She is the kind of woman who always puts an extra plate out at dinner in case a friend or a visitor happens to show up; the kind of woman who regularly takes pies and cakes and buns to the bachelor next door; and the kind of woman who, God willing, can cure whatever ails you.

Pauline's mother-in-law was a well-known Ukrainian midwife and folk healer. Pauline remembers that the sick and suffering would show up daily – there would always be four or five people sitting around the kitchen table – and the old woman would be on her hands and knees under the table, treating gangrene on their legs and feet and performing the traditional prayers on them.

Using her mother-in-law's cure for gangrene, Pauline tells me she, too, has saved many an appendage over the years. This specific panacea involves cooking the pods and stalks of poppies for three days on the stove to make a jelly, then applying the salve using heads of rye, while saying a special prayer to seal the wound. However, this recipe also includes 'laudin,' an herb used for incense in Ukrainian churches. Pauline says the laudin is difficult to order in from Ukraine, and is prohibitively expensive.

Hanchuk states in *The Word and Wax* that although folk medicine was widely practiced in Ukraine, locating the necessary and specific ingredients in the new homeland was hard. *"Old Country folk remedies required herbs, plasters, or other materials that were not easily obtainable,"* she writes. *"The wax ceremony, however, could be practiced readily by a healer armed with an appropriate incantation, water, and beeswax."*

I am about to experience the wax ceremony firsthand. Pauline is up at the counter. She cleans out a clear glass mixing bowl and fills it with water. As the wax is heating, she stands at the counter with her back to me, whispering prayers. She drops three separate dollops of wax into the water, then remarks, "Well, this has never happened to me before! You must be special." And she shows me that there are now four wax lumps in the water. She removes them and sets them on the counter.

Then she moves a chair to the middle of the kitchen for me to sit on, and stands behind me. She places her big warm hands – one on my forehead, one on top of my head – and begins whispering prayers in Ukrainian. There are lots of 'ch' and 'sh' sounds. At one point, she stops, leans forward and asks, "What's your name again?" Then she straightens up and resumes the foreign whispers, punctuated now with my name.

Moving around to face me, she brings the bowl of water to my lips so that I may drink from three different spots. Then she dips her hands in the water and anoints my forehead and cheeks, my throat – all the while whispering prayers in Ukrainian. She bends down in front of me and washes my bare knees, my shins, my ankles. And the ceremony is done.

We sit down at the kitchen table again. I feel cleansed, innocent . . . and hungry. Pauline wants me to eat. She fills my mug with more hot chocolate and sets a huge tin of homemade chocolate chip cookies in front of me. Then she walks over to the windowsill where, mellowing in the sun, are several green tomatoes and a big red one. She brings the ripe one over to me, cuts into it and insists I taste it. It tastes like summer.

The next thing I know, she's in the fridge pulling out things to accompany the tomato: fluffy white buns and thick cottage cheese handmade by the Hutterites, fresh butter, dill pickles. She slices up the rest of the tomato, brings over the salt and pepper. While I'm happily savouring the heady homemade flavours, she sits down with the wax clumps to interpret them. Turning each of them over in her big brown hands, she tells me that I've had a full life with lots of adventure (very true, sometimes I think a little *too* much adventure); she identifies that I don't like caves or things overtop of me (admittedly I'm fairly claustrophobic); she warns me to beware of certain people who are jealous of me and would want to hurt me (this is timely as I just messily extricated myself from a toxic friendship very recently and am still feeling raw and abused); and she correctly identifies a personal – and painful – part of my history. Then she fixes her dark eyes on mine and resolutely states that I am a good person and God is looking out for me. "Remember that," she says.

Her husband John ambles into the kitchen to get a cup of hot chocolate, and joins us at the table. He asks if I'm here for the myotherapy and I say, "What's myotherapy?" At which point I learn that Pauline is actually in high demand as a bodywork healer. People have come to her from Ontario, Alberta, B.C., Quebec, the U.S., and even New Zealand for her no-nonsense treatment. As she explains it, her healing touch is not about gently channeling universal energy, but instead, knowing intrinsically where the source of a problem is and giving that area some rather firm attention. She calls it myotherapy.

Pauline was first inspired by a healer named Leonard Gillinsky, of Bruno. John tells me he remembers working at the trainyards in Bruno when he was younger, and according to him: "People came from all over – the States, everywhere – to see Leonard. They'd come in on the #9 and #10 passenger trains. We used to carry them off the trains on stretchers, we'd take them down to the hotel, Leonard would give them treatment, and then they'd be back on the train. They'd leave their crutches, or whatever, behind."

Leonard saw something special in young Pauline by the time she was 11. He told her she had 'the feeling' in her hands, and that people were someday going to need her, so he mentored her. Pauline says that in Leonard's later years, a fellow in a wheelchair came up from the States to see him. American doctors had tried everything to fix this man's legs, but with no success. After Leonard treated him, he returned to the U.S. without his wheelchair. But soon after, says Pauline, the American doctors sued Leonard for practicing without a license. The financial and emotional toll pretty much ended Leonard's healing career. This was another valuable lesson from Leonard; Pauline got certified in both reflexology and massage.

Between John and Pauline there are many anecdotes that get tossed off in normal conversation. Like recently, she tells me, a group of Hutterites from High River, Alberta picked her up at 5 a.m., and drove until they arrived at their colony later that evening. They brought her to see one of their members, the head of a family, who hadn't been able to leave his bed for the past two years. Even his meals were brought to him there, says Pauline; he was in too much pain to move. Pauline gave him a treatment when she arrived the first night and one the next morning. That evening he came down and sat at the supper table with his family for the first time in two years. "His wife would sit at the table with her head down, she never looked up, she never smiled," says Pauline. "It had been hard on her, with him bedridden for so long. So he comes in and sits down on a chair, and when she looked up and saw him sitting there, she burst into tears. Since then, they have sent me the most beautiful rugs – here, I'll show you them." And she brings out a box with three colourfully patterned throw rugs. Several letters of thanks and gratitude fall out too, from other members of the colony she treated on that trip.

"I treat osteoporosis, sciatica, stomach ailments, colicky babies . . . whatever He sends me," she says, casting her eyes upward.

"I have such great power of believing that the Lord sends the people to me, and whatever has to be healed, He will protect me," explains Pauline. "There's people coming here with psoriasis you would never believe – leaking, running, flakes falling like wax. And one of my friends says, 'You've got to put rubber gloves on.' I said, 'You know, the Lord sends this person to me and He will protect me.' I have no fear. How can they contact me all the way from B.C. or Quebec or further on – the Northern Territories – how does this word or connection go if it isn't by the grace of God? So I don't worry about it. I'm ready when He takes me. When I had my heart surgery, I said, 'Dear Lord, if I come out of this I will work for you, I will not be fancy with my family, and I'll work anytime I'm needed.' So there are times I'm so tired I can hardly move, but I still have the strength to do a treatment – now there's something there. It's got to be the grace of God."

Just last week, says Pauline, she was in Spiritwood and performed 18 or 20 treatments in one day. Around 11 o'clock that night, she had finally finished. She sank, exhausted, into a chair and someone brought her a sandwich, some cookies, a cup of coffee. "But I had no strength to go and take that cup of coffee and put it to my mouth, I was so played out. How I would have loved to just take that coffee and drink it, but there was no strength to lift it. And a knock came on the door. And they told me so-and-so was here, he would like to talk to me. He came in with two canes, shuffling and barely moving his feet. He said, 'I just wanted you to take a look and see if you think maybe you could help me.' So I went to give him a treatment – I touched him and so help me, it was just like the first person of the day. I worked on him for, I think, two hours that night. And he came walking out with those canes hanging on his shoulder."

The phone rings a few times during our visit, with people wanting to come get healed by Pauline. At one point, she is in the living room speaking to someone on the line from Swift Current, and John shakes his head to me.

"The trouble with her is she can't refuse," he says. "They show up, can't walk in the goddamn door, they're crawling on their hands and knees . . . you can't turn them back."

* * *

As the summer progresses, I visit Pauline twice more, and both times she's occupied elsewhere when I first arrive. But it gives me a chance to get to know John, and two of their sons who still make it back to the farm regularly. By now, the blue heeler is no more; he ate a few of those fuzzy goslings and Pauline shot him. And the baby ducks were stolen right out of the horse trailer. But Pauline's son Willie has a good idea who might have taken them, and he plans to get them back.

On one occasion, Pauline offers me an 'ear-wicking' treatment. "I make my own wicks," she tells me, leading me into her tiny therapy room off the kitchen. "A lot of people don't even know they have this fluid build-up in their ears, but they may have problems with their balance." There is a narrow cot in the room; I lay on it, left side up and facing her.

"This," she says, showing me her homemade wick, "just draws the junk right up and out of the ear, it's so painless." The wick is about 11 inches long, and hollow like a straw. It's made of material (cotton, I think), covered in beeswax. It looks much like a candle, and the process is sometimes called ear-candling. I had tried it once before; it's supposed to remove wax and detritus from the ear.

The theory goes that once the candle is lit, the air in the straw warms up, forcing cooler air down one side and warmer air up the other side. A vacuum is created in the straw, and in the ear. This forces the warmed air into the ear and when it leaves, it draws out waste.

"So are your wicks the same as the ear candles in the health food stores?" I ask her while she's finding her matches and olive oil.

Pauline shakes her head and screws up her face in unreserved disapproval. "Those long ones they sell, they say put a plate under it if it drips – well, right there you know it's no darn good for you! The flame doesn't pull up," she explains. "It burns to the side because it's not the right wax, it's not the right material. You must use wax from an orchard," she informs me. "It's the only kind that doesn't drip. And there can't be a drip because the ear is very important."

She now places the wick in my left ear and lights the top end. There's a tickling in my ear, sounds of crackling and snapping. "The flame must be really flickering," instructs Pauline. "That's when it's starting to pull." I can feel that pull now, a pressure in my ear. "When people have fluid in their inner ear, you'll hear the 'crack-crack-crackling'," she says, "and when it burns wax, you'll hear a real 'whoomph'."

Once the wick burns down to a three-inch stub, she removes it and repeats the process on my other side. Afterward, she drops two beads of oil in each of my ears. "Never put anything in your ears," she warns me. "No Q-tips, nothing. If you ever have an earache, just put a little olive oil in your ear."

When she had finished, there was a new *consciousness* inside my ears. I could hear … bigger. This feeling – of more air, more space in my ears – lasted for days.

* * *

Another afternoon finds Pauline and John and me sitting around our mugs of hot chocolate at the kitchen table. I've been reading more about the wax ceremony. From *The Word and Wax*, I learn that: *"The cure often involves divining the source of the illness. The ceremony can also be perceived as a genre of oral literature, because it is always performed with an accompanying ritual prayer or incantation."*

Pauline agrees. She says she uses a different prayer for different conditions like nervous breakdowns, stuttering in children, fear, nightmares.

I ask her if many people come to the house for the wax ceremony anymore. "There's quite a number of people that still come for prayer, because there's not too many people doing it anymore," she says. "As you do the prayer, there are things involved. Like the water should be taken first thing in the morning from the well. And the first words have to start with Jesus Christ . . . Dear Jesus, Dear God."

I take a sip of my cocoa, and then ask her what the prayers mean in English. She's never translated them before, but she starts by closing her eyes and whispering the prayers in Ukrainian . . . then opens her eyes and translates: "Dear Jesus, heal this, change this and bless it with your blessings." She closes her eyes and there are more 'sh' and 'ch' mutterings.

John is now at the counter, opening and pouring an industrial-sized can of chocolate syrup into the hot chocolate machine. Pauline gets momentarily distracted watching him perform this task, but she soon shuts her eyes and resumes translating. "Where have you come in? From what did you come in? From priests, from gypsies. I am praying with you, not with my strength but the blessed mother. The loving, the caring, from her heart for this person," she turns to me, explaining, "you say their name," then closes her eyes and continues, "and from Ste. Anne, Ste. Verna, Ste. Madeline. I'm asking for your help, for you help all creations. And please have heart for . . . you say the name of the person you're praying for."

Here, it seems the prayer turns to banishing any evil presence, as Pauline intones: "Leave the house with the flame, out of the porch with smoke, and leave from the yard with the wind. Go to the nuisance grounds, where people throw garbage out – that's where you are recognized, that's where you were stoned and that's where they gave you your name."

Pauline opens her eyes. "And then you say, 'In the name of the Father, the Son and the Holy Spirit, Amen.' That's the first part." John has finished filling the dispenser and heads into the other room to check out the weather channel.

"After the wax is poured," she says, "you give them a drink of water from three places on that dish. And then you take the water and wash their face and the head." She whispers in Ukrainian. "And then you pray to cleanse their 'kostya,' that means their bones, veins. And you pray to cleanse their sinful flesh – because sometimes a person does go wrong – to protect them from certain evils going around, and bad winds. You wash the face three times and make the sign of the cross three times, then you wash over the chest, and then you do the top of the hands and the knees with the water."

Pauline's face brightens as she suddenly remembers there's something she wants me to try. 'Trucker Treats,' she calls them: these are dough ends deep-fried and sprinkled with sugar and cinnamon. She sets a bag of them in front of me, sits back down, and describes the remainder of the Ukrainian ritual; the prayers, and the pouring of the wax into water.

"Once you take the wax out and turn it upside down, you can see exactly what a person gets scared from," she says. "Not everybody can read it but sometimes it is very plain to see. Like if a child got scared from burying a grandfather or a father, it'll show a coffin going down a hole. It'll show caves, like maybe if you did a trip to the mountains and you were leery to go through and it held a bit of fear, that'll show. It'll show other people. It has also shown that a mother has given up her child and it's sort of floating away and she's grabbing for it. I've had people that have had abortions, it even shows that. And when people do evil to others, it will show in the wax. So, you can't hide too much from a person that can read it."

I nod while munching on Trucker Treats. I am seeing that the reading will be as subjective and as individualistic as the person interpreting the wax. And I know that Pauline brought as much to those four wax lumps as I did.

According to Hanchuk: *"The wax ceremony is a magico-religious and oral-incantational genre of folk medicine. Depending on the healer, the ceremony is invested with Christian as well as pre-Christian imagery . . . The oral formula contains religious and parareligious symbols. In order to bring about a cure, the healer fuses magic, religion, formula, and faith."*

Pauline's voice drops as she tells me one last crucial component. "For prayer, it really should be done before noon," she says. "From midnight 'til 12, that's the special time. And do you know, that's when your garden and everything grows? After noon, it all shuts down. You know the sun can be blistering hot and you wonder, 'How can a darn little plant grow?' But on a real nice evening where it has been good and warm during the day – if you ever have the privilege – once the sun sets, you sit real quiet and you can hear the plants rising and growing." With naked admiration she tells me, "You can hear them sort of *lifting*, coming out of the ground. If you're sensitive enough, and interested, you can hear them."

I'm smitten in that instant with this brawny woman who is completely comfortable on a tractor, a semi-trailer truck, or a front-end loader – caring so tenderly for these new little sprouts. I'm moved by the image of this indefatigable woman – always baking, cooking, farming, gardening, healing – taking the time to sit and listen to the soft, ethereal rustle of budding plants.

And I realize I got a lot more than I bargained for in Pauline: I went to see her for the wax ceremony, and learned that she was a highly sought-after bodyworker; I arrived with tape recorder and objectivity intact, and was soon barefoot and eating fresh tomatoes with her while swapping stories of being single children; I came to interview her about a specific folk ritual, and was let in on a whole world of folklore. I showed up as a stranger and left as a friend.

BEN E. DICTION

He is well-known through word-of-mouth, and through all sorts of people. I've been hearing about him for years; from a massage therapist in Saskatoon, an artist in Spiritwood, a rodeo rider in Big River. He is a legendary healer who lives up north. In fact *he* is the reason I first came up with the idea to create a book on Saskatchewan folk healers and diviners.

Problem is, he does not do formal interviews. And why should he? He certainly doesn't need the publicity. He's always booked solid with people wanting to see him, and now that he's 70 years old, I've heard he's thinking it's time to retire. He's been doing this for 35 years, says it's getting too hard on his body.

Interview or not, I still needed to meet this amazing man. And I still wanted to acknowledge him – honour him – by including my story of meeting him. I decided that, in order to respect his privacy, I would not use a tape recorder or camera. Nor would I publish his name and whereabouts.

When I phoned to book an appointment with him, I spoke to his adult daughter who gave me directions to their farm: drive west out of a northern town, four miles past the speed curve, then take the only grid going north, and drive two and a half miles. I did a little on-the-road figuring to transpose compass directions and miles, into left and right and kilometres – and was pleased I wasn't hopelessly urbanized when I pulled into their well-treed, well-kept and clearly well-loved farmyard. To the right (I mean 'south'), clean corrals flanked sturdy barns; to the north, colourful perennial beds set in green, tended lawns led to a welcoming white farmhouse.

His daughter greeted me at the front door and told the old shepherd-cross dog announcing my arrival to 'shush.' I took my shoes off, then stepped into the kitchen to sign a simple waiver at the table – aware of two little children shyly coming in to check me out – when the man himself ambled up to me smiling, extended his hand and invited me in. I followed him through a clean, open dining room, then turned right into a small side room. The treatment bed in the middle was surrounded by anatomy posters, books on everything from juicing to massage, a framed print of the Last Supper, and the Creator's Prayer ('Great Spirit, Let me not criticize another until I have walked a mile in his moccasins.') We chitchatted about my long drive today, how warm it was outside. He had gentlemanly manners, with the affectionate demeanour of an older relative. I liked the way he spoke: slowly and earnestly, with an up-and-down inflection that somehow reminded me of hitting my funny bone.

Then down to business; he was observing my structure, my posture. And I was free to observe him. He was wearing a white, short-sleeve cotton shirt – almost clinical – and the over-stitched, leather tie-up slippers my grandfather always wore. His hands were noteworthy in that he had very large, square, *friendly* fingernails. (For fun, I later checked in a palmistry text: these nails indicate a broad-minded, honest and clear thinker in good health). His blue eyes focused objectively one moment, then softened into twinkling smiles the next. The door to the room remained open; I could hear his daughter talking to her young children in the dining room.

"Just have a seat there on the side of the bed please, ma'am," he said, and sat in a chair beside the bed, facing me. "Now place your feet on top of mine, if you would, please." And I remembered that this was the unusual technique people mentioned when they spoke of this healer. I set my feet on his, wondering how he could feel my bare feet through his leather slippers. He was looking at my shoulders, my collarbones, my knees, my dangling shins.

Like a kindly patriarch tending to a bumped elbow, he was playfully grave as he said, "My girl, what happened to you when you were seven years old?"

I asked him if he meant physically or emotionally. (It was a banner year on both fronts).

He said, "Physically."

I told him I fell off a top bunk bed on my first night at summer camp and broke my left arm.

He nodded and informed me that injury is creating my lower back pain today.

"And what happened to your left foot when you were eleven?" he inquired, his eyebrows crinkling with warm concern.

"Hmm," I said, "once I stepped on a big steel rake, and two tines pretty much pierced through my left foot … but I was a little younger than eleven."

"Close enough," he winked. "And what did you do to yourself here?" he asked, lightly touching my right shin. I hiked up my pantleg to see if there was a scar there that might spark a memory. Nope. He said, "You walked hard into something a little lower than this treatment bed." I couldn't recall anything specific, but having lived a life coloured by all manner of cuts and bruises, I haven't kept track of every incident. I asked why he thought I'd been injured there; he said it was because he was sending that spot energy and it wanted more.

"My girl," he smiled gently, "what is bothering you, what brought you here today?"

"Well," I answered him, "it's mostly out of curiosity." I told him I was writing a book on folk healers, and that I'd heard of him lots and wanted to meet him. "But," I shrugged, "I don't have any real *problem* . . .," and then tears were suddenly spilling down my cheeks.

Now I readily experience life on an emotional level, but let it be known that I don't make a regular practice of crying in front of strangers. It's happened only a few times before in my life – when unchecked tears came so soon after meeting someone, and for no apparent reason. Looking back though, I do see a pattern. It has to do with an overwhelming reverence I've felt toward rare individuals who have a dynamic, palpable power – yet are gentle and humble.

He hastened to comfort me: "No worry, my girl, you don't need to tell me, we'll see if we can't make you feel better," and he handed me a tissue.

His face changed now; he was serious and focused. He rubbed his hands together, then cupped them and raised his arms above his head, while watching the space above me, around me. His hands were a couple of feet in front of me and slowly descending in a funneling way, creating almost an hourglass shape. He didn't look in my eyes. He was working with body energy now, connecting to the corporeal; observing as he went – my neck, my shoulders – the areas his hands were level with. I noticed his thumbs were drawing in towards his little fingers. He leaned forward in his chair as his hovering palms slowly descended in front of my shins. Smiling, he said, "Your legs are sure helping me out, my girl. They're doing just what I want them to." I didn't know what that meant, but I appreciated the encouragement.

His beautiful, four-year-old granddaughter brought in her laughing baby brother and they played quietly in the treatment room. It all felt very familial, very inclusive and safe. Periodically, Grandpa looked over at them and his face, serious with concentration, softened up completely as he winked at them. "That boy can do this, too, the best I've seen," he nodded over at his grandson. "He's got it real strong, I see it in him and feel it off of him."

Now bent over in his chair, his palms were hovering above my feet. Here he made a barely perceptible sign of the cross – moving his right hand up and down once, then left to right once – and sat up to look again at my collarbone, my shoulders, my knees. "And me," he added, "I got it from my grandma. It always skips a generation."

He placed both his thumbs on top of my wrist, fingers on the underside, and with tiny movements there were audible cracks underneath his fingers. He did the same to my other wrist. Same positioning, now on my knees. "See this?" he said as he manipulated my lower leg back and forth to show me the limited range of motion. 'Click, click' on the underside of my knee, then he gave the leg a push to prove it was now swinging much more freely. He was like a showman – a magician – with his smooth confidence, and before-and-after demonstrations.

"See the toes, how stiff they are?" he said, pressing his palm against my toes to stretch them back towards my shin. "We'll see if we can't make these toes happier," he grinned, and then a few clicks later – Ta Da! – they glided to and fro.

Now he moved his chair to sit perpendicular to my right leg, then lifted up my calf to rest on his knee. Palms up, his hands swept along beside my leg while his knee slowly elevated my leg. Down to the foot, he ended with another subtle sign of the cross. He moved over to my left side and repeated the process.

He asked me to lie on my side on the bed. "You're not pregnant, ma'am?"

"No," I assured him.

"And how old are you?"

"Thirty-eight."

Satisfied with the answers, he leaned in and gently stretched my shoulders and hips in opposite directions first on one side, then the other. He stepped back to look at the lay of my shoulders on the bed, then instructed me to lie on each side again while he gently pressed down for lower back cracks. "That moved good," he said, upbeat. He asked me to stand up, twist around a bit and see how everything felt.

"Not bad," I said, rotating my shoulders, "but still a little tight in the back ribs – maybe from the drive up today." I lay back down on the bed, he folded my arms across my chest, then reached underneath me and cracked my back over his supporting arm. Again I stood up and swiveled my shoulders and torso to check for pain.

"Feels good," I said, and I meant it.

I lay on the table and he placed his hands on my feet, pressing specific tender points firmly, but never so hard that I flinched. Then he set a vibrating machine under my feet for a massage, and flicked off the lightswitch in the room. "Okay, you can rest for a bit now," he said. "You earned it!" He swatted my shin affectionately, and walked out into the dining room.

The room was now tranquil with a soft luminescence muted by windowshades; the voices of the family gently drifted in from the other room. It reminded me of younger years, when an afternoon nap would incorporate the noises and goings-on from the rest of the house. It was reassuring and pleasant.

In a few minutes, he was back to check on me. "How do you feel, ma'am?"

"Good," I told him, "I feel really good." And then we got talking. About the thoroughbreds he breeds, and loves. About how he can see where these racehorses are hurting and send them energy – to their shoulder, to their hock. Even to lengthen their stride. He told me he'd been asked to go to Calgary with a horse trainer he knew; they'd give him his own trailer, pay for all his expenses.

"But I don't want to do that right now." His eyes stopped twinkling and clouded over. "My wife just died here in April and I'm not ready to be away from home." His beaming grandson, propelled by tippytoes, wheeled his mobile saucer into the room; Grandpa turned and laughed with him.

"Anyway my girl, let's see how you are." He turned the light back on, removed the massage machine, and asked me to sit up and swing my legs over the side of the bed again. He stood facing me, rubbed his hands together, then his palms were up and slowly descending to rescan my body. Around my shins, his right thumb was again pulling to the centre of his palm.

"See that thumb moving in?" he said. "I don't control that. That happens when the area still needs more energy." He explained to me that his left hand is the 'feeder'; it feeds energy to the person. He showed me three brown lines on his left hand, and told me the healing energy comes through those channels. His right hand, he said, is the 'drawer,' and it draws the negative energy from the person.

"Sometimes after working on people," he said, "especially if they're sick, my hands will be almost black."

He had finished scanning right down to my feet, and again he made a small sign of the cross with his right hand. I asked him if these were blessings. "Yes, ma'am," he smiled. "Because He's the one doing the work," he said, pointing to a wooden cross hanging on the wall. "I'm just helping out." He winked at me. Then I heard people arriving, talking to his daughter in the kitchen. I assumed his next appointment was here.

His daughter must have told him after our phone conversation that I had hoped to interview him on this visit, because he now proffered: "I'm sorry, my girl, I don't do interviews. Never have. I keep this as my little secret," he said, then laughed. "And I think people hear of me anyway." He wished me a safe journey home, and said "Bless you" as we shook hands good-bye.

I walked out of that cool and pleasant home with its generations of warm and friendly family . . . into the picture-perfect yard of flowers, lazy farm animals, grand old shady trees. And I wondered if people would some day be enjoying that same pastoral scene when they come for treatment from his grandson.

Myself, I had no particular ailments when I'd arrived that day; I couldn't say I had been healed. But in being treated by this man, one thing was for sure: I had been blessed.

ROOT WOMAN

T he house in the 'hood was once a screaming lime-green, and was known around Saskatoon for the bikers and drugs to be found there. Now it's an earthy mushroom-colour with sunflowers, carved wood pieces, and wind chimes gracing its oversized corner yard. Pressing the singsong doorbell brings Kahlee Keane smiling to the front porch, her blue eyes flashing beneath short-cropped silver hair. "Hey kiddo, come on in! I was so pleased to hear from you, I was wondering where you'd gotten to! Come in!"

I follow her on ceramic tiles through the living room, past a little wood-burning stove, and bookcases neatly stacked with texts and CDs. There is a medley of art on the walls, along with several framed black-and-white photos of Paul Robeson, Miles Davis and Fidel Castro – like family portraits affectionately displayed. Into the kitchen now with its open shelves housing jars of leaves and powders, coloured bottles of tinctures, containers of salves, bowls of drying berries. The handwritten labels read 'Juniper,' 'Licorice Root,' 'Stinging Nettle,' 'Labrador Tea,' 'Sage,' and 'Ratroot.'

Out the kitchen window, I see the back yard is still showing some green under the autumn yellow leaves. There's a little windowed greenhouse and more carved wood and clay figures. An open periwinkle-blue shed by the house looks like a summer kitchen; inside is a small stove underneath some big pots and overhead, herbs hang from clotheslines to dry. "Oh, the yard was a mess when we moved in," says Kahlee. "It was just dirt really, with broken beer bottles in it. Davey and I did a lot of work to get this place in shape, and I think we did a rather good job. It feels good now. It feels *right*, wouldn't you agree?"

I spent some time with Kahlee six years ago, when I took one of her weekend courses on Saskatchewan medicinal plants. Several times after that, she and I had tea and went on nature walks together. But within months, she returned to B.C. to be with her partner Dave, and we lost touch. She had entrusted me with 'Fledge,' a young grey owl which she had found years before freshly killed on a highway. She couldn't bear to leave the creature in that condition, so at great cost, she'd had him preserved. Forever in flight. In my basement.

Now, years later, I feel like I'm in an aunt's kitchen. "Yes," I say. "It does feel right."

The kettle is whistling. Kahlee shows me some corky-looking chunks sitting on the table. 'Chaga,' she tells me, is the name for this fungus that grows on the birch tree. "Oh, it's a *wonderful* creature," she gushes with a hint of English theatrics, and empties the kettle into the teapot. "It's been used by the Russians since the 16th century. In certain regions they drink it daily, like we do coffee and tea. And in those regions, there are dramatically lower rates of cancer. Chaga heals and strengthens the body, and has anti-tumour effects."

While nibbling a morsel of the dried mushroom, I silently recall a line from *Alice in Wonderland*: "One side will make you grow taller and the other side will make you grow shorter." I smile to myself.

Kahlee tells me she discovered chaga in the mid-80s, when she was living on an island off the coast of New Brunswick doing medicinal plant research. "I had what some would call a 'medicine dream,' and central to the dream was the clear image of chaga hugging the trunk of a white birch," she says, now pouring the peaty-looking brew into two teacups, complete with saucers. "It is my belief that this dream came as a reminder of buried knowledge, a rekindling and renewing of interest in the possibilities of this wild medicine."

She hands me a steaming cup, and I take a small sip of the bitter infusion. "It makes the loveliest tea," she says, encouragingly. "Very earthy tasting. And you can re-use the same piece of fungus over and over!" We sit down at the dining room table with our mushroom tea, and the conversation cascades, pools, and overflows. I feel like I'm in a film; Kahlee has always reminded me of Maude, played by the wonderful Ruth Gordon in *Harold and Maude*. It's a sweet story of friendship between a young man, depressed and alienated, and a 79-year-old woman with a zest for life and no rules at all. Like Maude, Kahlee is lively, irreverent, witty and warm. And there is no shortage of profanity.

We find ourselves on the subject of her past; she speaks with reticence. Kahlee was born in England, some 62 years ago. Her mother was a herbalist there, "although she did many things; herbs weren't her dedication at all." After the Second World War – "when Jews were *finally* allowed into Canada," Kahlee emphasizes scornfully – the family moved here. Her father was a manufacturer's representative so Kahlee spent her young years, with her parents and older siblings, driving back and forth across Canada, hauling a trailer. "We'd pull up somewhere, then start making dinner, and my mother would tell me to go collect this, go collect that … we'd have what I called a 'grass salad.' She'd first take out the things that were poisonous. I learned, from her, that kind of smartness."

However her family life hasn't left her with many good memories, so we move on to talk about books, personal health, my recent marriage, the Fates and our Higher Selves – and then we agree I'll come collect her Wednesday for a walk in the woods. Stepping out onto her front sidewalk, I turn to see her stick a large pink "Do Not Disturb" sign on the outside door and wink good-bye.

* * *

Wednesday afternoon, as I approach her front gate, Kahlee is already coming out the door with greetings and smiles. Dressed in festive-coloured layers and a jaunty tweed cap, she radiates the whimsy of going to a Tea

Party. These walks in nature are exciting to her; she gets to reunite with her plant friends.

I notice a medicinal plant, mullein, growing outside the fence on the streetfront. Its leaves are soft and velvety like lamb's ears, and I wonder aloud if such a tactile treasure wouldn't quickly get plucked up in this inner-city neighbourhood? But Kahlee says she wouldn't mind; her philosophy is that the plucker would subconsciously need that plant, in whatever way, to assist them. "That's how it works, kiddo," she says with a grin.

As I unlock the passenger door for her, she reaches in her day-pack and presents me with a book called *The Standing People: A Field Guide of Medicinal Plants for the Prairie Provinces*. It's a full-colour handbook she and Dave published in 2003, highlighting over 150 medicinal plants found on the prairies. I had been planning to purchase the manual at a local bookstore, so I insist on paying her for this unexpected copy. She refuses, saying it's a gift. And that is that.

We drive for half an hour through low hills ripe with autumnal blush, to Pike Lake Provincial Park. Ours is the only vehicle in the parking lot. It's the kind of overcast afternoon that is humming with stillness. Heavy with an unburst humidity. We stroll over to the river's edge and within minutes, there's a huge blue dragonfly clinging to Kahlee's index finger. It feels today like we are part of nature when it's not conscious of being watched; like being at the zoo once it's closed for the night. We stop to gaze at a beaver lodge across the water, and Kahlee starts telling me about her adopted mother, Madeline Thierault. Her Indian name was Wise Day Woman.

"I met her back in about 1985," says Kahlee. "She got hold of me when I was living in New Brunswick. She said she'd seen me in an article or something and that I looked like Rita MacNeil ... I guess she meant my *size*," she chuckles. "Anyway, she told me all about herself, she'd been a bush   Indian for half of her life and then moved to the city. But she said she felt a kinship with me, and she wanted to adopt me. I was already in my mid-40s by then, but I was thrilled. She gave me my name, 'Root Woman,' in an Ojibway ceremony."

It wasn't the first time Kahlee had been given the moniker. As a young woman, she had travelled all over North America, living with and learning from herbalists and healers, especially Native American and African American. The black healers in the South called her 'root woman,' as they do with people who have insight into the natural world. Years later, a group of Cree men she was working with in Saskatchewan spontaneously named her Root Woman ('ocepek iskwew') for her knowledge of the plants.

"Anyway, Madeline taught me an earthiness," Kahlee says, peering now at the dragonfly. "She taught me about the animals, all about the beavers. In her life, she'd been a keeper of beavers. She and her husband managed a beaver park on Bear Island." I am suddenly in my Grade 3 classroom, captivated as my teacher reads us *Paddy the Beaver*. Jeez, I'd forgotten those lovely Thornton Burgess stories. On this day, it would not surprise me to see Uncle Billy Possum or Peter Rabbit come-a-visiting their friend . . . .

"And I taught Madeline about medicines," continues Kahlee. "She used them, but didn't know the names, you know – she was like that. She died three years ago now, and just before she died, she said to me, 'Remember me; I'm of the Beaver Clan.' Davey and I came out here to do a ceremony just after her death and it was quite an amazing sight: the place was *alive* with beavers, they were crawling all over that lodge." As she gestures out to the water, the dragonfly's wings flicker with opalescence. "But since then, the beavers have left, they don't live there anymore. Now I believe it is a spirit lodge, and Madeline lives in it. She hugged the earth for a long time, and then she left. I felt very honoured to know her."

Kahlee places the dragonfly on a branch and we continue walking along the bushline of the riverbank. She brings out several dried cloves from her front jeans pocket, and we chew on them slowly while ambling. With a numb tongue I ask her how she came to know so much about herbs, what drew her down that path.

"The path was just there and I took it. It seemed absolutely right," she says, idly watching her hiking shoes kick up dry leaves. "I assume it is how one feels when they decide on their course of action at university. Or dare

I say in a religious vocation, for it's a very spiritual journey," she says with graceful elocution. "The path is multi-faceted, the connection with the Earth primordial. And the standing people communicate their intent when you become intimate with them."

In the introduction to *The Standing People: A Field Guide of Medicinal Plants for the Prairie Provinces,* Kahlee explains that First Nations teachings refer to plants and trees affectionately as 'the standing people,' each with a spirit. "They are there for we humans to utilize with a caretaker attitude," she says, thoughtfully. "If this is done, they open to you and actually become more potent in your embrace. So, I actually learned from the plants."

She stops and fixes glimmering eyes on me. "The trick was understanding and lifting the veil." A bird flutters up from the bush, and disappears into the grey atmosphere. The light changes – it seems brighter – although there is no suggestion of the sun in that opaque sky.

We are at the river's edge, and Kahlee points out stands of arrow-shaped leaves growing out of the shallow water. "That's the wapato, or Indian potato. If you dig under those leaves you'll find tubers, like little potatoes, down there in the mud. They're starchy and a little sweet, but the sugar in them can't be used by our bodies, so they're actually safe for diabetics. The Native women used to stand in the water and work them out with their toes," she muses.

Bubbles are surfacing amidst the pond lilies floating peacefully on top of the water. Kahlee tells me the water lily's root is used as a lung medicine, and that these roots can grow up to 80 pounds! I imagine a giant squid-like rhizome with tentacles on its squirming shoots . . . . We turn to leave the riverbank and its monstrous hidden treasures – *was that a 'glub-blub' I just heard behind me?* – and climb a knoll to stop at a sturdy bush covered in scarlet berries. "This is a high bush cranberry," she says, rubbing a stem between her fingers. "The bark is used to ease cramping. I've used it, it's very effective. Some people use the cranberries to make jams and jellies. I don't, though. The berries smell like dirty socks when they're cooking!"

Kahlee is now heading into the dense woods; I feel like I'm following the White Rabbit. We are soon enveloped under a living canopy of lush green leaves. Kahlee sticks out her smiling face and sings, "Hi, guys!" to the plants. We have arrived.

Like the hostess at a tea party, Kahlee starts introducing me to her friends, providing a personal anecdote with each new name. Within minutes, I've met Wild Mint: "In traditional medicine, the whole plant was used to treat indigestion, colic, diarrhea, and stomachache," Kahlee says and gently rubs a leaf to release its refreshing scent. Next I'm led over to meet Cow Parsnip whose seeds, I'm told, provide a local anesthetic for painful teeth and gums when nibbled on. And I soon find myself nodding an acknowledgement to Snakeroot: "Wherever the trouble lies, this medicine will find it," Kahlee states.

I ask Kahlee how she knows which plant medicine a person may need. She says that if she walks with them in nature, she can often find their medicine. "Nature is the ultimate backdrop to hear plant and man," she expounds. "The impressions are deeper, and the intuitions are heightened. So when I'm walking with someone that's ill, I'll step back and look at them in the context of the woods and I'll see medicines coming forth. Not always, but that does happen."

As an example, she reminds me of a young fellow who had also participated in the weekend workshop I took with her years ago. He had ankylosing spondylitis, arthritis of the spine. "You know," she says, "he leaned up against this tree and suddenly started talking about it. It was a birch tree, and we were all surprised by how much he knew. I realized *that's* his medicine. And really, the chemical constituents of the birch are exactly what was needed for his spine." She spent some months working with him, making plant medicines for him, and he reports that his disease has been in remission ever since.

We step lightly along the footpath, over roots, down into glens, across a wooden footbridge. Kahlee turns to me with those sparkling eyes and says, "It's *that* kind of a day, do you feel it?"

And I do. *'Curiouser and curiouser,'* keeps running through my mind.

I spot someone I recognize. I walk over and bend down for a closer look. "Leaves of three, let it be," warns Kahlee.

"Ah yes," I say. "Hello Poison Ivy."

Ivy's pal, Stinging Nettle, is also nearby. Kahlee uses nettle and other plants to help diagnose health problems. She once literally stumbled across the Devil's Club plant and discovered its spines could be scraped on the skin with any resulting inflammation indicating liver problems. "Devil's Club spine isn't a common tool, though. This is my own thing, kiddo," she adds as a caveat.

Kahlee eyes an old friend, then leads me over to Fireweed and touches it tenderly. "You know, in the German raids of 1940 and '41, much of London was pockmarked, grey and burnt. As a little girl, I remember a family scrapbook of those days that contained a newspaper photo of a gay wild plant, vigorously growing out of the ashes among the ruined buildings. That image flashes back every time I see a stand of fireweed, glorious fireweed, so loved by Londoners in need of a bit of beauty to heal the scars of war. And so needed by the Earth when fires have ravaged her Standing People."

"Pleased to meet you," I murmur humbly to the leggy stems.

Kahlee has helped all sorts of people throughout the years. Her gift is to walk with people in nature, and enable them to find and utilize their own medicine. This she does for free. But she doesn't call herself an herbalist in that she would never say, "Come to my office, I'll give you medicine for that, and it will cost such and such."

She does, however, proclaim herself – and loudly – an *eco*-herbalist. Through her dozen published books, her many years of writing a weekly column in Saskatoon's *Sunday Sun*, her school talks and frequent hands-on workshops, she is urgently trying to educate others to respect the fragile and endangered prairie ecosystem. In *The Standing People*, she lists 13 factors which are rapidly wiping out a number of native plant species; among them are clear-cutting, herbicides, pesticides, loss of habitat, global warming, pollution and commercial harvesting.

Kahlee and Dave represent an organization called Save Our Species (SOS), whose mandate is to educate the public in wildcrafting. Wildcrafting is "the ethical gathering of wild plant material for personal use by knowledgeable people." The group has very specific guidelines for harvesting plants, and designates certain species which need to be given a break to replenish themselves.

"I want to be a voice for the plants," says Kahlee, as we wend our way through the woods. "They can't speak for themselves and they're suffering. Right now I'm trying to save the Seneca; this is the plant that brought Dave and me back to Saskatchewan. It's been a loyal and good medicinal plant to many people through time. It was a major source of income for people during the Dirty Thirties and has always been used by the First Nations people. But these days it's being commercially harvested to the extent that its very existence is severely threatened," she says with disgust. "This is a plant that doesn't germinate from seed, it takes many years for the root to grow big enough for harvesting. The roots are sold on the international market; there are no regulations in place and no records of how many tons of Seneca are being shipped." I notice her eyes are moist. "I've wildcrafted it myself over the years for personal use, but it's time for all of us to quit digging this plant up. We need a moratorium on harvesting Seneca."

Her outrage now softens to simple sadness. Kahlee sighs that there is no heartwrenching footage of plant slaughter, like there is with whales or tigers, to incite public compassion and protection. "Plants are not cute and cuddly, and children don't grow up hugging little stuffed plant toys. But these species are the product of thousands, even millions, of years of evolution. And once lost," she says, shaking her head, "they cannot be regenerated."

We walk along in thoughtful silence until we come to the parking area where our lone vehicle waits. A huge tree directly in front of the paved lot is heavy with big, red berries. Kahlee stops and marvels that she has never noticed this mighty creature here before, especially because it is a species of hawthorn tree not native to Saskatchewan. She takes out a little plastic bag and starts plucking berries.

"There's been a frost," she explains, "so that's good. It changes the chemicals of the berries. Hawthorn is completely benign; an old person can take it, a baby can take it. It is a heart remedy. And our hearts are hurting so." Kahlee thanks the tree, then hands me the half-full bag of berries. "Here you go, kiddo," she smiles. *"Hawthorn for the heart."*

It takes me a moment to understand that she has found me my medicine. Heart disease is, indeed, my obvious genetic risk. It took my father when he was not much older than I am now. It is what I worry about in the middle of the night, or if I am feeling all alone.

She instructs me to take the berries home, place them in a jar, cover them with vodka, seal the jar, and in 14 days strain off the tincture into a bottle (I envision a whimsical, wee paper label on the bottle, reading *'DRINK ME');* then I am to sip a little elixir every morning.

As we drive back to town through the amber and russet landscape, I am awash with that cleansed and humble feeling of having just cried. It is part renewal, part gratitude, part hope.

And I realize my heart already feels different.

OF HARTMANN
GRIDS AND PYRAMIDS

Rhabdomancy: Divination by means of a wand or rod

His manufacturing business on the outskirts of Humboldt is just past the CASE tractor and John Deere dealerships, next to Morris Industries. I step into the cavernous, high-ceilinged warehouse, infused with the industrial smells of oil and metal, and wait for my eyes to adjust to the light. Then I spot Joe Menz; wearing a black CAT jacket and blue jeans, he's walking over to meet me. He's tall and lean, probably in his mid 60s. In fact, he looks like a handsomely-aged James Garner. He has the large, well-worn hands (minus one fingertip) of a hard-working fellow who knows his way around heavy machinery and construction sites. Joe quietly nods a greeting to me with deep brown eyes unwavering and honest … set in whites stained by a lot of life experience.

Joe's daughter, Donna, comes over to introduce herself; she is the company accountant. With her attractive facial features and warm brown eyes, she looks a lot like her father. They now invite me into their no-frills, concrete-floored office. As Donna moves to sit behind the desk, Joe pulls up a plastic chair for me. He then takes a seat in the corner, leans back and crosses one lanky leg over the other. Amid the harsh noise of grinders and drills, we chitchat about how Joe got into business. In the '70s he was a journeyman carpenter, but with four mouths to feed at home, he said he "needed to up his income." So he started Western Industries, manufacturing fifth-wheel campers; eventually he diversified into grain boxes, seed treaters, and now roll-covers for trucks. By the looks of things, he has done well.

But that isn't why I came to meet Joe. I'm here today because (and this he had told me over the phone, with a shy chuckle) Joe is "ready to come out." He is ready to talk publicly about his real passion, his life's purpose; and he is prepared for the inevitable skepticism. You see, this man's man is actually a rhabdomancer, a bio-locater, a water witch … a dowser.

Dowsing is a form of divining, and divining is the art of accessing information not available to the five senses. It's an ancient art. References to dowsing can be found as far back as 1556, in a book by Georgius Agricola called *De re Metallica*, in which Agricola writes of some people's ability to discover underground veins of ore using a forked twig.

Typically, a dowser will hold a tree branch or a metal rod in each hand, and walk over an area to locate underground water, minerals, oil, land-mines, lost objects, and more. When the branch pulls downward, or the rod turns 90 degrees, whatever is being sought is directly below the dowser.

"So did you have a natural gift for dowsing?" I ask Joe.

"Yes," says Joe. "I dowsed when I was a kid. I helped people find water on their land . . . but I quit doing it. Then in '71, we bought a property and needed a well. I shouldn't even tell you how I dowsed for that one," he laughs. "Do you know what a crowbar is?" I nod. "Well, I held a crowbar balanced in my hand, and walked. When the crowbar went down, I dug there!" He shakes his head. "But there is still water there to this day."

However, he again quit dowsing after that episode. I get the impression that Joe is a solid type of guy who is not comfortable with anything that might be considered New Age or flaky. And although he has occasionally pulled out his dowsing rods when it was essential to find water – a man's gotta do what a man's gotta do – he hasn't spent a lot of time musing about the mysteries of dowsing. Until the day he found something with his rods that resonated with him personally and changed his life: geopathic lines. Joe had located earth energy.

Joe tells me that geopathic lines have been studied extensively in Europe and have consistently been shown to promote cancer, MS, chronic fatigue syndrome and other immuno-related conditions in people living over them. Donna is nodding enthusiastically, while organizing a large pile of papers in front of her on the desk. In fact, Joe says, in Germany they dowse all land slated for development before building on top of it. However, in North America, he says, we don't even believe that the earth has its own energy . . . and we do not question the alarming patterns of disease in people who live in certain locations.

"The way we all got into this," Joe explains somberly, "it was eight years ago, my wife was ill and we went to see this German holistic doctor in Kelowna and he told her that there was geopath energy running through our home. He was the one that told us that they do not build a home in Germany until they check for these negative or harmful lines first. Anyway, at the time I thought it was all garbage. But I got thinking about it and ironically I thought, 'Well, I used to dowse for water . . . .' So I got my trusty L-rods out and of course I did pick up something in our house – I didn't know what I was picking up. That's when Donna started to do research."

"At first," says Donna, "we thought dowsing was just looking for water. But we've since found out that you have to say specifically what you're looking for. When we first came across all this, we found it very hard to believe. But the more research we did, the more we found that knowledge of geopath energy is very common. More people knew about it than we had thought."

She hands me a paper to read. On it is a quote from *The Sacred Earth* by Brian Leigh Molyneaux: *"In China, the primal power of the dragon was said to be channeled through the landscape along paths of energy 'dragon lines.' These lines were regarded as very auspicious locations and used by members of the imperial family as burial sites. Locating the way in which the flow of energy, both positive and negative, interacted with the landscape was developed into a highly sophisticated practice, geomancy, which is still used today."*

"This is also really big in Europe," says Donna, "in England, Ireland, Scotland, Germany. They've found that a lot of the ancient temples and megaliths like Stonehenge were built on sites with these positive 'ley lines' running underneath. In England," she adds, "they refer to geopathic energy as ley lines. So some of this energy is positive, but some is negative. And it's the negative lines that Joe dowses for."

"But what is geopathic energy?" I ask, needing to start this story back a few steps (I *knew* I should have taken more sciences in high school). "Like, why would it hurt humans? Wouldn't it be natural?"

Joe is clearly more comfortable, more articulate even, when speaking of the science of earth energy, the mechanics of it. "Geopathic stress consists of extremely high frequency radiation that is out of the range of ordinary meters," he says in a measured, professorial tone. "It disrupts the body's electrical field and its electrical control systems. What we're working with, I feel, has a lot to do with our levels of diseases such as cancer."

Donna, meanwhile, has found an official definition in her papers to answer my question. "Okay, this is according to Dr. Joseph Mercola," she reads aloud: "Geopathic stress is natural radiation which rises up through the earth and is distorted by weak electro-magnetic fields created by subterranean running water, certain mineral concentrations, fault lines and underground cavities. The wavelengths of the natural radiation disturbed in this way become harmful to living organisms. Electropathological energy created by modern technology can also contribute to geopathic stress in the form of high and low frequency energy from telecommunication towers, electricity pylons, transformers, radar and radio towers." She looks up to me. "Dr. Mercola is a naturopathic doctor in Illinois," she adds.

"You see," Joe explains, "our body, our brain signals work on 7.83 hertz, or cycles, per second. Being on a strong stress line or geopath line can increase that to 250 hertz or cycles per second. Now it's been proven that anything over 180 hertz I believe it is," he says looking over at Donna for confirmation, "causes big trouble."

"Yes," Donna says, "in the 1930's, the U.S. scientist George Lakowsky showed that humans and animals have less chance of fighting bacteria, viruses and parasites at frequencies above 180 hertz."

Joe looks back to me. "I like to think of that as if you ever have a radio on and it's working beautifully, then somebody comes along and it starts to crackle – it has a frequency interruption, it's not working. I think that's what's happening with the geopath lines to our brain signals."

"O-kaaay," I say slowly, trying to process this information. I realize my forehead is furrowed and I'm frowning. And speaking of electrical disruptions, my tape recorder is suddenly on the fritz, erratically stopping and starting. *That's odd,* I think, then get out my pen and start taking notes.

"So this can cause MS and cancer?" I ask, a little doubtful.

"It's not actually the negative lines that are *causing* the sickness," Donna says, quick to correct me. "It's the fact that they interfere with your immune system, your body can't heal itself. So we believe once the negative lines are neutralized, then your medications or vitamins or whatever you're on have a chance to fully work with your body. It's not that neutralizing the negative lines will cure you; it's that it helps your body to cure itself, with everything else you've been prescribed. Basically this is the ground level, this is the base. Other therapies won't work if you're being badly affected by geopathic energy."

Donna starts leafing through her stack of research, all the while explaining, "There are different sources of harmful energy that can affect the body and one is, oddly enough, the water lines. Here it is," she says, and removes a page from the pile, then reads it to me: "In January of 1929, German scientist Baron Gustav von Pohl, a talented dowser who believed that earth radiation affected tree growth, animal behaviour and human health, set out to officially prove that cancer deaths only occurred in people who had been sleeping in beds positioned above a powerful underground water vein. In collaboration with the Berlin Centre for Cancer Research, Baron von Pohl dowsed and recorded his findings in the town of Vilsbiburg in Southern Germany. The scientist mapped earth energy lines in the town, then compared them to the records of the district hospital. It was found that every one of the 48 recently recorded cancer deaths had occurred in people who had been sleeping in beds standing exactly above one of the powerful water veins Pohl had mapped before seeing the medical records."

"Really!" I exclaim. This is a completely new world to me . . . .

Donna looks up, nodding. "Yes, water is a harmful source of energy when it's underground," she says. "Another is something called the Hartmann Grid, which was discovered by a geobiologist named Dr. Ernst Hartmann." She pulls up a page showing lines running in a cross-hatch pattern. "Those lines run north and south, east and west. And this is a quote from Dr. Hartmann: 'Cancer is a disease of location triggered off by geopathic stress. We all produce cancerous cells on a regular basis, but they are continuously destroyed by our body's immune system. Geopathic stress does not cause cancer, but weakens our immune system.'

"And then there's the Curry Net, and those lines runs diagonal – they go north-northeast, and south-southwest ... right, Joe?" she asks, now looking over at her father. He nods in affirmation. "Right," she continues, "and the Curry lines have different intensity, but they are usually on top of the Hartmann Grid." She procures a document heavy with text, points to a paragraph and states, "In fact, Egon Pohl proved to the Central Committee for Cancer Research in Berlin 60 years ago that one was unlikely to get cancer unless one spent some time in a geopathically stressed place, especially when sleeping."

I ask what the sleeping connection is. Donna starts to answer, then finds the sheet that, she says, explains it better. She hands it to me. Joe excuses himself at this point, to step outside for a cigarette.

I settle back and read *Geopathic Stress (GS),* by Rolf Gordon. Gordon has been studying geopathic stress since his son died of cancer more than 20 years ago. He has dowsed thousands of homes whose owners had developed cancer, and found consistently that crossing earth energies below where the bed is situated will cause cancer. For instance, he detected two lines meeting at the head of a bed, and the resident there had a brain tumour. He discovered two lines crossing in the middle of a bed whose resident, it was revealed, had cervical cancer. *"The one square metre you sleep on and therefore spend about one third of your life on, must be free from Geopathic Stress,"* he writes. *"During sleep, your brain does your body's 'housekeeping' including creating 80 per cent of your new cells, giving the right signals for your body to operate properly and absorb the correct level of vitamins and minerals together with adjusting hormone balance. GS will interfere with this process and leave your immune system weak. All these body functions will usually become normal very quickly after GS has cleared out of your system."*

His book, *Are You Sleeping In a Safe Place?* chronicles years of investigation which have led him to make this claim: *"One is unlikely to develop cancer unless one has slept or stayed for long periods in Geopathic Stress places."*

I look up to see Joe has quietly returned and is sitting in his chair. "And you can find this geopathic stress under the earth?" I ask him.

"Yes," he states firmly. "Dowsing gives you what you ask for. So I started asking for geopath energy lines – and I've been getting them." He quietly, respectfully, tells me a story about dowsing the home of a local elderly couple after they'd both died of disease. Joe said he found a distinct line running through their bed; one that would have crossed under the heart region of one person, and the head region of the other. Indeed, one died of heart disease and the other of a brain tumour.

"Wow," I respond softly.

"Yes," says Donna, "you can research a house and see patterns of disease. And they say that's why the gypsies were always healthy, because they moved from place to place. They never had any diseases. Except alcoholism," she adds, jokingly. "So they say when you buy a home, check the history of the previous people – did they have cancer? That's something to look for."

"I'd like to dowse this whole town," Joe says thoughtfully, "and map it out, showing all the geopath energy lines. I don't feel comfortable dowsing for illness per se, although people have asked me to. I feel very strongly that my powers are with earth energy. I'll tell you if you have geopath energy and where, but you need to figure out how those lines coming through would be affecting certain family members.

"And the worst place to be is where any lines cross – that's called a vortex. Oh, and speaking of a vortex," he says, remembering something, "I should show you this." He stands up and opens a drawer of the metal filing cabinet beside him, then hands me a drawing of a circle with numerous lines running through it, all meeting in the middle. It looks like a bicycle wheel with many spokes.

"That," he says, "is a crop circle, if you can believe it." Donna now tells me a crop circle appeared around Humboldt in about 2004, and out of curiosity, Joe had taken his L-rods out to the field and dowsed it. As far as crop circles go, she says, this one was apparently unusual in that the field lay in a counter-clockwise pattern.

"Ironically, up until this crop circle in Humboldt, I don't think anyone had dowsed one," says Joe. "I was the first one to dowse it. And I found the crop circle had a multitude of lines all crossing in the middle. And in my mind, all this negative energy came in here and created that swirl. That's just my theory. I think it was formed from the pulling of the energy, from the vortex."

"This crop circle happened to have negative energy because of the spin," says Donna. "But there's crop circles with a clockwise spin that people go into and feel really good in. We had people come out here to investigate it, one stood in the centre taking pictures and one stood on the outside taking pictures. But when they went home, the one in the centre found that none of her pictures turned out – and that is documented on their website."

The website is that of Beata Van Berkom, a volunteer researcher with the Canadian Crop Circle Research Network, which investigates and reports all Canadian crop circle activity. "Mostly I get a very pleasant and uplifting feeling from the formations," Van Berkom reported on her website. "I did, however, encounter a circle at Humboldt in the 2004 season which apparently had many 'Curry' lines running through it and it had a very ill effect on me. People felt a lot of heat from it. It had a lot of power, I couldn't even stand up straight in it. It also broke its share of compasses."

BLT Research, a group of dedicated scientists and fieldworkers, has conducted the most comprehensive testing on crop circles in North America. According to their website, electronic equipment failure is a regular occurrence around crop circles; cellphones won't work inside the circle but resume outside it, digital and film cameras fail to capture any images (sometimes breaking altogether), and TV cameras have commonly malfunctioned when called out to document a new circle. This could be due to remnant radiation caused by "an intense and complex energy system which emits heat (possibly microwaves) along with highly unusual electrical pulses and strong magnetic fields."

Freddy Silva, one of the world's leading experts on crop circles, writes: "And like all sacred sites, temples and places of worship – such as Gothic cathedrals – the crop circles appear at the intersecting points of the Earth's magnetic pathways of energy."

I ponder Joe's drawing of the vortex at the centre of the crop circle, then ask him why this circle suddenly appeared on one certain day when the geopathic lines had always been running underneath it. He tells me that some earth energy lines move; that, like the tides, they are affected by the cycles of the moon.

Now I'm envisioning this underground net of negative energy lines crisscrossing and creeping . . . stealthy and potentially lethal. "So once you find these lines, what can be done about them?" I ask. "Because you found these running through your house, too!"

"Well, at one time they used what they called 'earth acupuncture'," says Joe, "meaning that if you did find the line, you would drive a steel rod into the ground to divert it."

"It's the same as body acupuncture," adds Donna. "You have negative energies running through the body and when they put the needle in, they're diverting those negative energies."

"So back when my wife was ill, I did drive a bunch of stakes outside the house where I thought the lines were," Joe continues, "and it did neutralize the geopath energy. But then a year later, that same Kelowna doctor came out with this device called the Envirosphere, which he sold to us at a nice price," he says, laughing a little sarcastically. "I still thought it was garbage – at that time, anyway. But we did place it in our home, and did some more research on it. So one day I thought, 'Well, I'm going to see what this Envirosphere is really doing.' I took it off the line about six feet, and it did *not* neutralize the energy, my rods were picking up the geo. I put the Envirosphere back on, and it neutralized it." He says he took a hammer and smashed the object open, curious what was in it. After discovering the contents, he got Donna to do some more research.

"And that's when I came up with the pyramid," he states.

Donna now plucks out a page from her pile, and – as a quick introduction to the concept of pyramids – tells me about Dan Davidson, a physicist, and Joe Parr, an electronics engineer. As board members of the Great Pyramid of Giza Research Association, they have been experimenting with pyramid shapes in their labs for over 20 years. And they have shown that the pyramid shape produces an energy field which can block out known electromagnetic radiation and other forms of energy.

Joe, meanwhile, had walked out into the shop area and now returns with a four-sided pyramid object which he places on the desk in front of me. The pyramid is about five inches high, opaque black with silver flecking throughout. I pick it up carefully; it weighs several pounds.

"You combine the geometrics of a pyramid with what's inside this to enhance the effectiveness," says Joe. "The pyramid, no matter where you place it in your home, will neutralize geopath energy. It will neutralize all electromagnetic frequencies that you get from your computer, your lights, all of that."

I'm staring at the object, nodding. Joe sits back down in his chair, leans back and crosses one leg over the other.

"I'll never forget the first pyramid I made," he says. "Made it one afternoon, we placed it where it's supposed to be, and then I got my wires and thought, 'What's gonna happen?' Well … it worked! I explain to people that this is much like a filter. It draws in the bad energy, purifies it, then disperses it out as good energy. Ironically, some of the product we use in the pyramids is scrap from my shop – aluminum filings."

"Everything happens for a reason," Donna chimes in, smiling.

"Another thing we use in the pyramid is copper," says Joe. "There are 27 inches of copper wire coiled in there, clockwise, from the bottom up. Brass is good, too. Gold is the best," he admits, "but that would cost too much. Also we use double-terminated quartz crystals from Brazil. I use five of them in a pyramid – one pointing up, then one facing in each direction. The aluminum and the resin I use, it draws the negative energy and cleans it, then the crystals disperse it out in the right spin, a counter-clockwise spin."

He invites me to follow him out of the office to the shop area. There he shows me a handmade pyramid mold, and demonstrates how he puts all the ingredients together in the mold with resin.

"And there's a few other things in there that I keep to myself," he adds coyly. "But the main component is intention. That is the biggest factor. I have to be in the right frame of mind to make a pyramid – intention is most important. Normally when I do make my pyramids, I'll miss Sunday services, come here, close the door, and I'm more-or-less into a special mode. No disruptions. And that's the way I talk to God!"

Joe now brings out a smaller pyramid, about two inches high, and hands it to me to look at. "I did a test yesterday," he says, "and this little pyramid neutralizes up to 60 feet. This is the pyramid I use for vehicles, to neutralize electromagnetic energy. People sit in cars all day and electromagnetics hurt your immune system, disrupt the signals to your brain. Actually, there was a lady in here this morning, she's on the road every day, she was just telling me, 'You know Joe, that pyramid is a godsend, I'm doing two days work now where it used to take me three or four days.' She used to be exhausted, but now she says she comes home and she feels good. She says she swears by it."

Donna prods him to bring out some other testimonials from people he has helped. There are thank-you cards and letters: I see one from a Native healer, addressing Joe as a fellow healer; and another from a family in

Edmonton who write that their health and behaviour problems have completely disappeared since they placed a pyramid in their home to neutralize geopathic stress.

"Without exaggerating, I've made 100-plus pyramids," says Joe. "But the pyramids are preventative, too. Once you have one, it's good for a lifetime."

Hmm, I still can't visualize this whole geopathic energy thing, and the pyramids neutralizing it . . . Joe must sense that, because he now gets an idea. He asks if I have time to come over to his brother's new place in town; Joe dowsed the yard already and found earth energy, so he can show me there how the pyramid works.

"Yes!" I say, excited. "If you have time to show me, that would be awesome." Donna offers to ride in my truck and direct me over to her uncle's place; Joe takes his own vehicle.

It's only a few blocks away. As Joe gets out of his truck, I see he has his L-rods with him. They are made of black wire the gauge of a clotheshanger-wire and are formed into strong, straight 'L' shapes. He leads me over to the back yard, and gives me a dowsing demonstration. Knowing that there's obviously a water line somewhere under the ground, he says aloud, "Show me water," then slowly starts walking a straight line the width of the yard. His hands are loosely out in front, palms facing him at chest level, with the rods resting over top his index finger knuckles, long sides pointing forward. The short part of the rod hooks in front of the palm for balance. His gaze is directly ahead at eye-level as he takes slow methodical steps forward. I walk alongside him, scrutinizing those rods bouncing lightly over top of his fingers. At one specific point, the rods rapidly turn in. His muscles, his fingers, had not even twitched. He walks the width again, with his rods instantly pulling in at the same spot.

"See, so that's how it works," he says, pointing out where the water line would run up to the house. He tucks the rods into his back pocket. "Here try these, see if they work for you," and he gives me my own set of metal L-rods, then helps me position them lightly in my hands. They flop around, I have a hard time getting them to balance over top of my fingers.

I ask the rods to show me water, then I walk the yard looking directly ahead at eye level. Besides the clumsy jostling I haven't been able to get under control, there is no movement of the rods. They seem unresponsive in my fingers. I'm disappointed that I can't do it, but Joe chuckles and says that's okay. He says I can practice at home by tossing a penny out into the yard without watching where it falls, then ask for it and dowse to find it.

"They say anybody can dowse," Donna says, a little sardonically, and then tells me her own failures in trying to divine by dowsing. "And they say it doesn't take practice, but it does. It's like building muscles, you have to build it, then keep at it."

"I use my rods everyday," states Joe. "The rods are your antennae. You can ask them for whatever you want."

He brings his rods out of his back pocket again. "And if I ask for geopath energy, then that's what the rods will find." He now walks the long length of the yard and his rods quickly swivel at a certain place.

"So that's where the geo is. Now if I place a pyramid somewhere in the yard, watch what happens." And he walks over to his truck, brings out a 12-inch cardboard box housing a large pyramid, then places the pyramid on the ground near the driveway. He raises his rods up to chest position, asks aloud for geopathic energy, and stoically walks the length of the yard. Walking along beside him, I see that there is no response from the rods. He repeats it – again no movement.

"Interesting," I say, now with some conviction. I still don't fully understand this whole concept of earth energy and pyramids and crystals, but I trust Joe and I've seen with my own eyes the obvious reactions of his dowsing rods. I smile at him appreciatively. He walks back over to the pyramid, puts it back in the box, then hands me the box. As a gift.

I thank him in earnest; he suggests I put the pyramid by my computer when I get home. "Yes, I will …," I say, now dragging my sentence out before it's time for me to leave. There was something else I wanted to ask him before I go.

"So Joe, if you can ask for anything when you're dowsing, why not ask for gold or diamonds?"

Joe laughs and says, "I was wondering when you were going to ask that! But you cannot benefit from dowsing, you can't do it for greed. You must do it to help others, not to gain personally.

"Although," he adds, looking at me intently, "I really have gained from it personally. Since I started working with this, it has changed me big time," he says. "Working with this energy, I learned that we are *all* energy-based. And it's important that we think positive thoughts. I used to be so nervous, excited. Now I'm calm. I look at things totally different. Problems don't bother me as much as they used to. This is all within the last three years."

Donna emphatically confirms that her father is a much different man than he used to be.

"I am much more spiritual now," says Joe quietly. "I come from the old school, where you had to go to church every Sunday." He grins. "Now I find I can talk to God just going out to the backyard!"

I put all my new goodies in my truck, and we say good-bye. As I leave the outskirts of Humboldt, I remember another passage I read in one of Donna's sheets. It is by Joey Korn, a dowser and author. He wrote: *"Dowsing gives us the ability to explore the unseen world of the subtle but powerful energies that are hidden behind all of life. When you dowse for water, you're really detecting the energy field of the water rather than the physical water. Since everything is ultimately energy, everything can be dowsed. With dowsing, you can explore and unlock the secrets of the universe."*

I glance over at my new L-rods resting on the passenger seat. And I now see the resemblance: they look like a large pair of Allen keys. To *"explore and unlock the secrets of the universe."*

Or at least, perhaps, to loosen a few screws and get a glimpse inside.

LUMINOUS MYSTERIES

It's a drizzly, autumn evening in Saskatoon. As my truck slowly idles along a suburban crescent, I squint to make out the numbered addresses on the shadowy houses. This is a semi-rural area of the city, with '50s-style bungalows on oversized lots. I'm surprised how quiet and dark it is out here; there seems to be only one streetlight per block. On the last stretch of houses before the wide-open prairie, sudden signs of life; several vehicles squeeze past me, and the gravel shoulders are filled with parked cars. Through my foggy side window I see huddled shapes hurrying up a certain driveway. Must be the right place I figure, and pull over to park. I wrap my raincoat tight around me, then jog up the driveway to the rear of the house. In the backyard I pass a lighted, three-foot wooden grotto housing the Virgin Mary – her head gently tilted to the side, eyes cast down and arms outstretched in supplication. Several steps beyond is a two-car garage; the sign on its door reads, "Come In."

The welcoming space is alive with warmth and light and singing. There are some 60 people sitting in a semi-circle of rows facing the front corner where there's a long table, draped in light-blue material and covered with religious items: a wooden cross, an open Bible, figurines of Jesus and Mary, and several candles. I take a seat near the back on a white plastic lawn chair fitted with a square of grey carpet for padding.

In front of the altar, a woman stands singing. She is casually dressed in a yellow fleece vest, black cargo pants and black running shoes. Reading glasses hang on a string around her neck. Her long, dark ponytail gleams in the light as she turns to notice me. Then, continuing to lead the group in song, she walks over to a 'Help Yourself' counter, picks up a string of rosary beads and a pink, palm-sized leaflet of rosary prayers, and delivers them to me. As her mouth sings "Come Holy Spirit," her lucent brown eyes communicate to me in their own language. They say, 'Hey, glad you could make it!'

I feel somewhat conspicuous for not having my own beads, and for not knowing the rosary – for not even being Catholic – but I am pleased with her helpful gesture to include me. I watch her return to face the centre of this prayer group she calls the 'Marian Cenacle.' She looks so down-to-earth, so . . . normal. And I guess she is.

Carmen Humphrey is 53 years old, a mother of two boys, a registered nurse who is now retired and does some casual aesthetic services like leg-waxing out of her home. She is happily married to her second husband, her first marriage long ago annulled. Having met Carmen once before, what struck me most about her was her sense of humour. She has the affable qualities of being quick-witted and spunky, yet self-deprecating – kind of like a stand-up comedian. But this unassuming housewife from suburbia is, in fact, a renowned faith healer; a woman who is repeatedly able to facilitate, or as she would say *witness*, miracles.

Carmen is in such high demand as a speaker and healer that getting in touch with her took some persistence. The first time I called she was in Toronto for a week; the second time I tried she was in Quebec; eventually I did manage to see her a few days before she led a spiritual pilgrimage to the village of Medjugorje in Bosnia-Herzegovina. Now she's just returned from three weeks in England and Ireland. Regardless of her popularity, she is adamant that it is Jesus who does the healing – not her – and she has encouraged me to come to her Tuesday night Cenacle to speak with members of the group who've had first-hand experience of this phenomenon.

Briefly I look around at the many different faces here tonight. Although most of these people would be in their 50s, 60s, and 70s, there are also some younger ones. Amid the sense of veneration in this room, there is also an informality and the comfortable feel of community. Carmen now sits in a chair off to the side of the front altar while pre-selected people recite prayers, followed by the group's response. I join in the litany, thanks to my *Pocket Rosary Prayers.*

The booklet provides me with instructions on how to pray the rosary. The beads are divided into five sections, or decades, of ten beads each; these decades represent a mystery or event in the life of Jesus. There are four potential themes of rosary mysteries – joyful, luminous, sorrowful, and glorious – to reflect on while using the beads to keep track of prayers. Ten Hail Mary's count off the ten decade beads, with the Our Father, the Glory Be and the O My Jesus prayers punctuating between decades.

Tonight we will be going through the five Luminous Mysteries. Someone announces the first one; we are to meditate on "submission to God's will." I smile, remembering Carmen's entertaining tales of the crazy things that happened to her before she finally submitted to God's will. Carmen's chronicles are compelling because she had never dreamed she would be a conduit to God. She wasn't born into this, she was not groomed for this, she did not feel worthy of this. In fact, she described herself previously as "a stay-at-home mom who never goes anywhere, never does anything, never sees anybody." Having grown up in the French community of Bellevue, Saskatchewan, she had always been a practicing Catholic, sure. But there were times, she admits, when she didn't get to church as often as she should have, and there were bleak and tough times, too, when she even thought God had abandoned her.

However, on July 13, 1997, extraordinary events started taking place in Carmen's life. In those first confusing – even frightening – days, she thought she was losing her mind. Several acquaintances, as well as some strangers, shocked her by spontaneously telling her that they could feel the Holy Spirit was manifest with her. Meanwhile, a visionary visiting from Vancouver told her God had a mission for her. On a whim Carmen purchased a religious medallion, but when she showed it to a friend, it burned the woman's hand. Notably throughout that time, Carmen's own hands began tingling and itching almost unbearably.

"I started feeling a sensation in my hands, pins and needles and a real numbness on the inside of my hands," she says. "I started thinking, 'Oh my goodness, I'm going to have a stroke! I'm over 40 and I'm overweight; I'm going to die.'"

Furthermore, during this period whenever Carmen was in the company of someone suffering from any type of malady – there was a deaf boy, and another child with allergies – she would hear an unmistakable voice telling her to place her hands on these people and pray with them. She ignored this instruction; it was too socially bizarre to touch strangers and pray for them.

"I'm an RN you know, analytical, professional," she had explained to me. "So I'm thinking that there's no bloody way this is happening because this is not normal," she said, laughing with the memory. "I studied physics, biology, physiology, mathematics – two plus two is always four! I can't *believe* any of this stuff."

But inexplicable things kept happening. One morning at 2 a.m., Carmen was impelled to get out of bed and go to the kitchen. There she found a piece of paper and within two minutes had written on it a beautiful prayer, composed of words and expressions she'd never before used in her life. Soon after, she went to church and prayed: "God, I don't believe you would do this to me . . . I need proof. I need a sign. I don't want people to make fun of you and I don't want to be made a fool of. I need a sign and it's going to have to be a pretty big sign, a slap-in-the-face kind of sign."

The next day found her at her sons' school in a line-up with another mother, who told Carmen she was having a terrible summer; the arthritis in her left shoulder had prevented her from doing housework or even wearing her wedding rings for years. Carmen shocked herself by offering to pray with the woman. The two then found a space behind a classroom door and awkwardly prayed together. This out-of-character behaviour so unnerved Carmen that she went to her priest for counsel. And he stunned her by telling her that God had clearly given her the gift of healing hands. He also gave her the combination to the church lock, so she could come in anytime.

Days later, the woman with arthritis found Carmen again. "She comes running up to me and says, 'I've been trying to get hold of you,'" recounts Carmen. "I said, 'What?' She said, 'I'm healed!' I said, 'What do you mean you're healed?' She was raising her arm up and down. Again she said, 'I'm healed!' I thought, 'This is a pretty big sign.' I said, 'You'd better thank God for this because He's the one who healed you. I can't heal anybody. Only God can do that!'

"The next morning," Carmen continues, "I went back to the church and I said, 'Okay God, I believe you. If I don't believe you, I'm a fool.' I said, 'And I'm willing to do this, but I don't know how I'm going to do this. You're going to have to do it for me because I'm not going to stand on the corner of the street and touch people as they go by.'"

Within 11 months, she'd prayed over 1,500 people and in doing so, she says, witnessed 150 miracles. "I kept a record of the bigger healings I saw at first," she notes. "Then I decided not to write names down anymore because this is God's business, and all the glory should go to God. He's the one doing this. But there were countless healings: cancers, headaches, relationships, flu symptoms, diarrhea, constipation, depression, back pain – not a week would go by without my seeing a miracle. And to see a tumour disappear right before your very eyes . . . it just blows my mind. I'm still in awe every time it happens."

In my lawn chair, I now lean slightly to the left to see that Carmen is still sitting up by the altar looking nonchalant and relaxed, chewing gum. Smiling to myself, I muse on Carmen's forthrightness about what an unlikely character she is to be God's instrument of healing.

"You know," she had said to me, "I always thought God was scraping the bottom of the barrel when He came and got me," and we'd laughed. I had then asked her how this has changed her life. She was thoughtful before answering. "I was always the fun-loving one, the life of the party, quick with a joke. So when this happened, I lost all my friends except for three," she admitted, a little dolefully. "But you know," she'd added, shrugging, "I just find drinking is not so much fun anymore."

I settle back into my chair thinking, *Compared to witnessing miracles, I should think not!* Peering down at my neighbour's hands, I see he is holding the last bead on the first segment of the rosary. I find the same place on my string and intone, along with the group, the Fatima Prayer.

O my Jesus, forgive us our sins, save us from the fires of hell and lead all souls to heaven, especially those most in need of Your Mercy.

The decade of the second Luminous Mystery is the time to reflect on "devotion to Mary." We start with the Lord's Prayer, the only one of these prayers I know off by heart. I take this opportunity to study some of the faces around the room, hoping to recognize Francesca Iosca-Pagnin. I've seen Francesca's photo on the cover of her book, *Reflections 'Npink*, and I know she is a regular at this prayer group. Her book describes her harrowing experience with breast cancer. The writing is eloquent and brave, and imbued with a grace that made me want to meet this woman; to clasp her hand – just as a fellow, mortal human. As I'd read her journal entries I could remember what was happening on those dates in my own life, while in the same city Francesca was fighting for hers.

In early March 2001, Francesca had made the traumatic decision to have her left breast removed. She had survived breast cancer seven years earlier, but a biopsy in February had indicated it was back. Four days before her scheduled mastectomy, Francesca's friend invited her to Saturday evening Mass at St. John Bosco church. "She had arranged for a woman by the name of Carmen to pray over me after Mass," Francesca recounts. "She had heard from a co-worker about Carmen, a visionary with the gift of healing hands."

Francesca had first taken off her coat – she was told she might get very warm – and then Carmen prayed over her, blessing her with healing water that had come from Lourdes, in France. When she was finished, Carmen said she'd had a vision while praying, of the Blessed Virgin Mary scooping out the cancer from Francesca's body. "Calmly, yet tearfully," writes Francesca, "Carmen astounded me by saying: 'The Blessed Virgin Mary is going to heal you.'"

Francesca was admitted to the hospital on the morning of her surgery, but her surgeon met with her before the operation with more bad news. Her pre-op blood tests were indicating the cancer might have already metastasized to the liver and bone. If the disease had spread that far, her doctor said, there was no need to amputate the breast. At that point, Francesca stated to her doctor and family, "There's nothing wrong with me. Any further test results will come back negative . . . Mother Mary has already done the surgery."

The following morning, she awoke at 4 a.m. unusually relaxed. As she lay in bed, she prayed the rosary. "A strange thing began to happen," she journals. "A heavy current of electricity started to enfold and envelop my body beginning with my toes and moving slowly upward. My eyes were open. I was fully awake. At the end of the second decade, no sooner had I whispered the phrase about Jesus' blood than the slow, pre-meditated, magnetic electrical surge recurred. This time I noticed the current was deliberate and even warmer. This rolling wave of incredible energy stopped precisely under my breasts as if it were programmed to do just that. The same thing happened with the third decade. By the fourth, I was weeping as I prayed. At the end of the fourth decade, the methodical surge of electricity went up over my breasts, paused briefly, and then traveled out through my arms and fingertips. By the fifth decade, I was overwhelmed by bewilderment and awe and a sense of, 'My God, what has just taken place.'"

Although Francesca firmly believed she had been healed, she went through with the surgery. This was her second bout with breast cancer, and she had too much to live for to take any chances. But she refused the recommended chemotherapy as follow-up treatment. She had faith that God was looking after her.

Two days after the surgery, Carmen came to the hospital to visit Francesca. Francesca writes: "She showed me the rosary that she had been praying on for me since the beginning of the month. Originally, the links of the rosary were silver; now many of them were gold. The beads were blue when the rosary was purchased; now they were visibly darkening. Without question, the rosary was going through a metamorphosis. Carmen explained that she prays devoutly to the Madonna of Medjugorje and that rosaries changing colour is a phenomenon of Medjugorje."

It was in that Yugoslavian village in 1981, that the Virgin Mary apparently presented herself before six children and gave them messages. "These visionaries," writes Francesca, "testify that she continues to appear regularly, inviting pilgrims to peace, faith, conversion, fasting, and prayer. Mary, Queen of Peace, told the visionaries that the reason rosaries and medals change colours is to show that prayer can change human hearts, human endeavours, and human circumstance."

After Francesca's mastectomy, a pathology test was performed on the amputated breast. The report confirmed that, although the initial biopsy had shown cancer, the breast had, in fact, been cancer-free one month later when it was removed.

"The power of God's Holy Spirit touched my body and with His Boundless Love, bathed it with a heat that healed every molecule, every atom, every cell of my being," Francesca records. "I have come to realize with great sadness that I will probably never again experience that all-consuming, blissful, electrifying, deliberate surge of warmth I felt on that morning, but the grandeur and rapture of that day is never far from my mind and spirit."

I do not see Francesca here tonight. Now I notice Carmen give a small nod to a woman sitting a few rows up from me, who then recites the first phrases of the 'Hail Mary,' and the group finishes it. After the tenth time, I'm positive I will never forget these words:

Holy Mary, Mother of God, pray for us sinners, now and at the hour of our death. Amen.

My neighbour's hands have moved to the bead between the second and third decades, so I do the same. We're on the Third Mystery, which is about the "grace of conversion." I recall one person who is forever converted: Dwayne Bowkowy. It's not that Dwayne wasn't always Catholic, but he's the first to admit that there were some years where he strayed pretty far from the church. "Let's put it this way," he told me bluntly when I met with him and his wife: "I'm no angel!"

I'd recently had coffee with Dwayne and Maureen, to ask him about being healed by Carmen. Dwayne was a big, robust, outgoing fellow in his mid 50s. Maureen was a lovely woman with an honest visage, who was more quiet and demure than her gregarious husband. We chose a table by the front window of the coffee shop, hung up our coats, and sat down to talk. Dwayne told me that in 2001, he had started having dramatic health problems and was diagnosed with atrial fibrillation. "A-fib it's called," he said. "My heart would go anywhere from 29 beats to 230, just like that," he said, snapping his fingers. "They thought I was gonna have a stroke. I was taking 240 pills a month. Since 2001, I progressively got worse and worse."

We all leaned back from the table when the server brought our drinks over: mochaccinos covered in whipped cream for Dwayne and me, and herbal tea for Maureen.

"I was off work for eight months," Dwayne resumed his story. "I'd be in the hospital two times a month, for three or four days." He licked whipped cream off his spoon. "Oh yeah, and my heart stopped eight different times," he said, seeming almost surprised himself. "The last time it stopped for over a minute. They took me away and they said, 'He's in God's hands,' then they hauled Maureen away and that was it. When I woke up, there were 13 guys around me. I thought I was dead, that I'd went to heaven already – or maybe to hell, I don't know!"

Maureen giggled at him.

"Meanwhile, daughter heard about Carmen having these prayer groups and the gift of healing hands," said Dwayne. "She said, 'Why don't you go see her,' so Maureen give her a call and we went there."

"Well, first Carmen prayed for him over the phone," Maureen politely interjected, "and she told him, 'You're going to feel . . . .'"

"All warm and tingly," Dwayne jumped in enthusiastically, "or all warm and fuzzy for lack of a better term. And I did, I got flushed, too. She had said, 'Go somewhere it's quiet,' so I'd went in my room, I shut the door, I put the phone down and let her do her thing, it took around five minutes. And it felt all warm and nice, like you were in a hot shower."

"He felt better after that," said Maureen, "and then we went to her prayer group and she prayed over him."

"Hands on, yeah," nodded Dwayne.

That night, when he got home, Dwayne said he felt good for the first time in many months. He didn't feel sick, he didn't feel tired – and as a bonus, the bursitis in his shoulder was also gone.

"Yeah, Carmen fixed my shoulder *with* my heart," stated Dwayne, unequivocally. "Because I was scheduled for surgery on my shoulder, and she says, 'Lord, while you're at work healing his heart, fix his left shoulder.' And I'd had no movement there – to take a shower, to wash my hair, I couldn't do this," Dwayne said, now bringing both hands up to his head to simulate rubbing shampoo, "or I'd be passed out with pain. I never golfed for a whole year; I couldn't do it, the pain was unbearable."

"We got home that night and he was sitting in his recliner, and he said, 'I feel good. I feel like I did before I got sick,'" Maureen reaffirmed softly. "And then he went to scratch his head and he realized he could move that side."

"I said, 'Well Jesus fixed my shoulder through Carmen,'" said Dwayne.

"Because Carmen doesn't take credit herself," Maureen explained to me. "And when Carmen prayed, she had asked for a healing, or for the doctors to find a medication to help," Maureen said. "So after that he was still on his medication, and for three years he was good – no episodes. Then he did go for surgery a year ago."

Dwayne nodded, took a swig of his mochaccino, then set the cup back on the table. "But the *back*," he announced emphatically, "the back was the best healing!" And he launched into the story of how, one winter, he'd slipped on some ice and banged his head on a planter. At the hospital, after his head was stitched up and X-rays done on his back, the doctors forewarned him he'd be bruised and sore for a good week or two.

"This was a Monday," he said. "I'll never forget that because Tuesday was Carmen's prayer group and Maureen said, 'You'd better stay at home.' I says, 'No, I think I gotta go.' So, very slowly I shuffled my way in there, and sat right next to the door. The lady beside me was gonna give me the whatfor because I was moving all around, I couldn't find a comfortable spot, everything hurt so bad. It came to the part where Carmen does her healing for everybody. She says that while we were doing the rosary, Jesus told her to bring me up in front of the group, there was going to be a healing. So she put her hand on my back, and it was very, very hot. And she said her prayer – nothing – and I went back to the chair. And I was just sitting there, but soon I started moving around, then I bent down and touched my toes. And then I says, 'Carmen, I have to interrupt,' and I jumped up in the air and did jumping jacks, and there were a hundred people there and they'd seen what shape I was in. And I had *no* bruising, *no* black and blue!" Dwayne shook his head, disbelieving. "Yeah, that was the best one. It was just like right now; Jesus said there was going to be a healing and there was."

"Yes, Carmen calls him her 'miracle man'," Maureen laughed lightly, "because so many have seen him healed."

I smiled. "So have you had more healings?" I asked Dwayne. He was using his spoon to scrape whipped cream from the insides of the cup.

"Well, there was one time he had a toothache," Maureen began, "he'd been suffering for over a week . . . ."

Dwayne set his spoon down and snorted, cynically. "Yeah, went to the dentist, he said, 'Oh take some of these pills.' Well, you know where I could have put them, they didn't do any good."

Maureen looked tenderly at Dwayne as she explained: "They took X-rays, they couldn't find anything. But he couldn't even eat, it hurt him so bad."

"I took Tylenol 3 and ibuprofen and all this," said Dwayne. "Nothing could get rid of the pain. Went to Carmen . . . ."

"This was in her house," Maureen added, "and she said, 'Someone here is having problems with a tooth.' So he raised his hand," she nodded in Dwayne's direction, "and she prayed over it, and it was gone, too." She gazed at her husband, then she looked back to me and softly explained, "He didn't like to say anything because he thought he was being greedy and piggish, but Carmen said, 'You know, if God doesn't want you to have that healing, He won't give it, so don't be afraid to ask.'"

"Yeah," piped up Dwayne, "well 'Ask and you shall receive.' But like I ask, 'Why me?'" he said, shrugging in earnest. "Why do I get so many healings when the ones that are dying of cancer or this and that – they don't get one? My problems are menial, little. Like why me? But they say, 'He does it in His own way, in His own time.' I don't know if it's for me to get more strength for my faith, or . . . ."

"Or for others to see it," Maureen suggested. We three shook our heads at the imponderability of it all, and looked out at the autumn leaves fluttering under the streetlights.

Dwayne turned back to me. "I still don't see how people can't believe in Him – like I've experienced it, I relate to it. But if you haven't experienced it or seen it, I guess it would be hard to believe that there's a supreme being." Dwayne drained his mug and set it on the table with a sense of conclusiveness. Maureen and I agreed with him by finishing off our own beverages.

Tonight I see Dwayne and Maureen are sitting six rows ahead of me in Carmen's garage, over to the right. Their heads are bowed in quiet contemplation.

Here we move past the third decade of beads. I follow along with my *Pocket Rosary* and chant:

Glory be to the Father, and to the Son, and to the Holy Spirit. As it was in the beginning, is now, and ever shall be, world without end. Amen.

The prayer group is on the Fourth Mystery, we are to ponder "the Transfiguration and its spiritual fruit: courage." That image, this concept, triggers a lump in my throat as I recall the first time I met Carmen.

It was when Joanie, the mother of one of my best friends, Jennifer, was in the Intensive Care Unit at the University Hospital. Joanie had just moved back to Saskatoon a few months previous after many years living on Vancouver Island. Besides old friends and new grandchildren, what had brought her back to the prairies was a rapidly degenerating lung condition which had been worsened by the damp coastal air.

I paid several visits to Joanie in her riverside apartment over the summer. Although we always planned to go outside for a walk, she hadn't enough energy to leave her suite. By this time, Joanie lived with thick translucent tubes up her nose and a constant canister of oxygen at her side. During those visits we spent a lot of time talking about the different folk healers I was in the process of interviewing, and discussed whether any of those people might be able to help Joanie.

For 25 years, I had known and admired Joanie for being a non-conformist feminist hippie, a fierce human rights advocate who'd grown up in the Bronx in a labour-organizing, non-religious Jewish family. While her life's work was grounded in grassroots social and community work, she'd always had a strong connection to the magic and spirit in everyday life. And Joanie (maybe moreso in the past several years) believed in miracles.

As the summer progressed however, there grew a feeling of gravity and exigency; even with her oxygen levels now turned up to maximum, Joanie was no longer getting enough air. Although she'd held out hope to someday receive a lung transplant, it was too late and she was too weak. Her doctors could do nothing more for her.

So it was that she asked if I could arrange for her to see Carmen, the Catholic faith healer.

I phoned Carmen and told her about my ailing friend; Carmen said she'd be able to come pray with her sometime during the next week or two. Within days however, Joanie was rushed to Emergency, then was moved into the ICU. At this point, my friend Jennifer flew up from Washington, D.C. and she and her brother Sean took up vigil by their mother's bed. I contacted Carmen again and told her Joanie had taken a sudden turn for the worse; Carmen said she'd get up to the ICU as soon as she could.

The next morning, Jennifer and Sean were informed by her doctors that Joanie had no hope of leaving the hospital. Meanwhile, Carmen called to tell me she would come pray with Joanie that afternoon. When they heard a Catholic faith healer was now on her way to their mother's bedside, Jennifer and Sean seemed somewhat bewildered. They're both very scientific, practical people – at ease in the erudite worlds of law and molecular biology – and they had just been given the devastating decree that their mother was going to die.

Carmen arrived, appearing calm and comfortable. For years, she'd worked this ward as a nurse; she seemed indifferent to all the scary-looking tubes and machines. There was no sense of urgency about her, no polite hand-wringing or low-voiced concern over the state of Joanie, who was now mostly unconscious. Carmen stepped over some wires, then stood by Joanie's shoulder and gently touched her small arm. Joanie's eyes fluttered open and she looked up with alarm at this strange woman leaning over her. I quickly stepped up and explained to Joanie that this was Carmen, the Catholic faith healer she'd wanted to pray with her. Joanie nodded and closed her eyes.

"What's your mother's name?" Carmen asked Jennifer.

"Joanie," replied Jen.

Carmen looked down at Joanie's frail body heaving rhythmically as the huge mask covering her face forced air into her. "What's her condition, what does she have?" Carmen asked softly, perhaps more from a nurse's perspective.

Jennifer looked hesitant, I could see she was deliberating over something. Later she told me she was reluctant to tell the faith healer what her mother's incurable and terminal disease was in case that squelched the faint prospect of a miracle. Reticently she answered, "Idiopathic pulmonary fibrosis."

"Oh . . .," Carmen responded sympathetically to Jennifer, then she looked over to Sean, then gazed down at Joanie.

Suddenly quizzical, Carmen piped up: "What religion is she?" I wondered then if the thick black curly hair, olive skin and Roman noses of this family were alerting her to something . . . maybe unfamiliar.

"She's Jewish," stated Jen. "Not practicing, I wouldn't say."

Carmen's eyebrows raised in surprise. "Well does she know I'm Catholic?"

"Yes," I interjected. "And she asked me to ask you to come pray with her."

Jennifer motioned that Carmen should minister to her mother. "She wanted your prayer, so go ahead."

Carmen looked bemused, but she graciously complied. All I remember about the prayer is that Carmen asked Jesus to open His arms to Joanie. Standing beside her adult children, I thought I sensed them wincing a little. Maybe they felt their mother had forgotten her roots. Maybe they felt she was grasping at straws. Maybe they simply couldn't reconcile the doctor's definitive prognosis with this prayer of hope. But myself, I felt I was witnessing something special.

After her prayer, Carmen had lifted a little clear plastic bottle of water from her front pocket. She opened the cap, turned the bottle upside down, and dabbed some water from her fingers onto Joanie's forehead. She was cleansing Joanie, blessing Joanie, with this sacred water from the River Jordan.

When Carmen was finished, she wished Jen and Sean the best; we thanked her and she left. I could hear her moving down the hall and visiting with her old nursing pals.

We three stood there momentarily in the midst of vague questions, some obvious ironies and a general sense of, "Well . . . what now?" However, this family's indomitable spirit always shines through with sarcastic humour. Sean, who is well-traveled, gave an incredulous snort. "Have you ever *seen* the Jordan River?" he whispered to us. "It is one of *the* most polluted sites in all of Asia." He shook his head. "Man, if nothing else kills her, that water certainly will!" And we chuckled, grateful for the levity.

Joanie died two days later. But I do believe that asking for Carmen to pray with her in those last moments was an act of courage, of expansion. While her physical body was contracting and diminishing, her spirit was growing. At the end, I saw Joanie was all-encompassing enough to transcend any earthly labels and limitations. And too, here had been this hitherto stranger – Carmen, who owed nothing to Joanie and indeed had a vastly different view of God and morality and life – praying like a trouper for her. I was moved by a fragile and profound beauty in that whole event. I hoped Jen and Sean someday would be, too.

As for transfiguring, well two days later Joanie was a hummingbird . . . but that's another story.

Smiling now, I look around the garage to see where we're at.

Come Holy Spirit, come by the means of the powerful intercession of the Immaculate Heart of Mary, Your well-beloved spouse.

We've reached the fifth decade, the last segment of beads. This final mystery is all about the institution of the Eucharist – the consecrated bread and wine taken at Communion. The bread, or the Host, represents the body of Christ, while the wine is symbolic of His blood. Catholics believe that Christ is present in the Eucharist, and that this is His constant sacrifice and gift with which He nourishes the human soul. We are to meditate, in thanksgiving, on the spiritual fruit of the Eucharist.

O Sacrament most Holy, O Sacrament Divine, all Praise and all Thanksgiving be every moment Thine!

"I go to the Eucharist," Carmen had told me, "and I try to go every day, but I'm not a perfect person so that doesn't always happen," she said. "You know, life happens – there's appointments to get to, and groceries, and housecleaning, and you know how it is," she had said, rolling her eyes in resignation. "But I go because I *need* Jesus to come inside me and make me stronger. I need that reinforcement every day to purify my heart, to make my heart more like his."

Her brown eyes had been penetrating, sincere. "Because I am not perfect," she had assured me, shaking her head for emphasis. "I'm so ordinary, I'm just like you."

I see my neighbour has now bunched the rosary beads up in his hand; the prayers are complete. Carmen stands up to face the group, like a solo act taking the stage. Her hands are clasped together in front of her, but come apart frequently to gesticulate as she speaks. I'm entertained before she even says anything, she's got such great presence. Her reading glasses are on, but she takes them off periodically for added effect.

"As most of you know, we just got back last week from a trip across 'the Pond'," she says, looking intently at each of the faces on the right side of the room. "We were invited to all sorts of places – places with cool names like 'Glengormley' and 'Swords'." She looks around to the faces on the left side of the room. "'Ballykelly'." She smiles and makes eye contact with each of the people in the centre of the rows.

"And of course, we also went to London, and to Dublin – in Ireland I spoke in front of *800 people*," she says, her eyes twinkling and wide with mock terror. "But I gave two talks there in Belfast," she continues, "and the second group I spoke to was mixed, there were non-Catholics at that one. Because you know," she says, peering at us over the top of her glasses, "not everyone in Ireland is Catholic!" Her deliberate understatement draws some laughter from around the room.

She goes on to say that as a result of her talk, a young woman claimed to be healed of lifelong depression, while another boy was instantly rid of his disabling allergies.

"And this one woman had just had a mastectomy, her left arm was so swollen," says Carmen, her right hand hovering above her left arm six inches to illustrate the severity, "and her hand was just like a balloon! Anyway, I prayed over her. Then the next morning I went to church to get a little quiet time," she says, frowning to show the futility of that, "and she was there. She came right over to me and she said, 'Look at my arm, look at my arm!'" says Carmen, waving her left arm in the air, eyes alight with excitement. She then lowers her arm and loosely folds her hands together. "Her arm and her hand were not swollen anymore. So praise be to God," she nods her head, reverently.

"Praise be to God," intones the group in response.

After her informal talk is over, Carmen extends an open invitation for people to come up and receive prayer from her. This is not the same, though, as being 'called up' for a healing. I see that this is more of a visiting time; time for individuals to speak to Carmen, ask her if she's heard about this Sunday's special event at the church, mention someone in their family who is sick and ask her to pray for them. She bows her head with each person, says a brief prayer inviting Jesus to heal all suffering, dabs some holy water from the Dead Sea on the person's forehead, and makes the sign of the cross.

Several people stay after the Cenacle to help tidy the garage until next week. While we stack lawn chairs, I ask Carmen about long-distance healing; I've seen many of these miracles recorded on her website, and one time I'd been on the phone with her when a woman called from Trinidad to pray with her. For Carmen, the answer is simple: prayer has no limits and no geographical boundaries.

"Like I got a call last month from a man in New Brunswick, he hadn't been able to eat anything but bland foods for four years because of acid stomach problems," she says. "I prayed for him on the phone, and he called back just today to tell me he'd had a huge healing – he was so happy. He said, 'I can eat everything a *pig* can eat! Tell the world!'" she laughed. And she told me of a woman in another province, a friend of a friend, who had pancreatic cancer. Unbeknownst to this woman, Carmen had recently prayed for her. "I've never met her," Carmen states to me. "All I know is she was healed completely."

"Can you tell," I wonder, "when a person has been healed? Like can you feel when it's working?"

We've stacked the chairs to the end of the row, so we both stand up. "I can feel a liberation sometimes," she replies. "I don't know what is being healed or who is being healed, because I usually pray over a person's family tree – so it could be one of their ancestors 200 years back being healed."

"Really!" I say, surprised by this. But we have no more time to explore this now. A few remaining Cenacle-goers are waiting around to speak with her yet tonight.

Before turning to them, Carmen reiterates to me: "I'm not a healer, you know. This is not about me. It's about God and prayer."

And I believe her. I remember that when I lived in Montreal, I was so amazed by the fabulous French cathedrals. Of course, one is dazzled by the glorious gold domes and the ornate stained-glass windows and the gleaming wood in those centuries-old basilicas. But in many of them, their most unforgettable feature was their front entrance. The walls there would be hung with dozens of crutches, canes and wheelchairs; physical aids no longer needed after a faith healing had taken place. This was where the crippled had hobbled up to, where the infirm had been wheeled into – and this was where they had walked independently out of. Those walls were such a fantastic monument to the curative power of prayer.

Tonight I'm heartened to realize that such miracles don't have to take place in a magnificent church in a historic city in front of a huge congregation. Those same phenomena are happening quietly in grassroots locales on the homely prairies. They're happening daily in lowly places like school hallways, grocery store parking lots and backyard garages.

I gather my things, then step out into the dark night. The rain has stopped and the wet black pavement is shining brightly with the reflection from the lone nearby streetlight.

THE BOXER

This cold January morning, I'm standing outside a middle-class, two-storey home on an older Regina crescent, waiting for Joyce. It's because of me that she has an appointment in five minutes with the healer who lives here. Joyce's son, Greg, has been one of my closest friends since we were teenagers. Last time I saw Joyce was in August, when Greg was visiting his parents for a week, and I'd gone over to their house after interviewing Lee Donison – the healer Joyce will see today. I remember I was animated from meeting Lee, excited by his amazing abilities. I must have been convincing; Greg had immediately picked up the phone and made this appointment for his mother to see Lee. For me, that summer day had been an inspiration; I'm hoping this winter one will be for Joyce.

* * *

Five months ago, I had pulled up in front of the same house, unsure of who I was about to meet. His name had come my way several times, and always with obvious veneration. I'd been told that Lee Donison had saved many people's lives, cured incurable conditions; I'd been told he has 'magical' hands.

Indeed his hands had made him famous in Saskatchewan, although not for healing. In the 1950s and '60s, Lee was a formidable amateur fighter. He won the Provincial Heavyweight Wrestling Championship each year from 1953 to 1956. As a boxer he won seven provincial titles, both in light-heavyweight and heavyweight. In 1963, he won both the provincial and national light-heavyweight boxing championships. In fact, he is the first athlete in Canada to win provincial titles in both wrestling and boxing four times. In 1982, he was inducted into the Saskatchewan Sports Hall of Fame.

Heading into that first interview, I was aware of my own stereotype of a champion fighter. Although I can appreciate the strength and finesse of a boxer, 'the sweet science' is simply too violent for me. My stomach roils when one mighty punch brings a powerful man crashing straight down.

It seemed incongruous for a fighting man – a person who had once pummeled others into pain, injury and defeat – to now be an esteemed healer. So who the heck was this Lee Donison? Mohammed Ali with a complex understanding of anatomical pathology? Mike Tyson with a compassionate, intuitive spirit? The pieces wouldn't fit together for me.

From the outside, his brick house was pleasantly shaded by mature trees, but revealed little information. I rang the doorbell and was let in by a stately woman in her 60s (his wife, I assumed) who briefly instructed me to take my shoes off and have a seat around the corner in the living room; he was with someone else at the moment. Then she was gone. The living room was imbued with the formality of a parlour, albeit an eclectic one. There was a statue of the Virgin Mary, some Inuit art, several Ukrainian-style embroidered and framed pictures, and a large Balinese carved wooden trunk. In the midst of it all, there was a three-foot-high iron stand which cradled a glass ball and churned out rainbow-coloured mist into the room – this curio was right out of *Lord of the Rings*! And it all served to further confuse any notion of who Lee Donison might be.

I heard a door on the other side of the hall open, then a young woman saying 'good-bye' as she left by the front door. A smallish fellow peered around the corner – *was this him?* – and quietly invited me to follow him into the treatment room. Well here was no macho thug but rather, a shy and soft-spoken man. He was maybe five-foot-eight, compact and well-built, with a full head of salt-and-pepper hair. Looking very spry and hale for a man in his late 70s, to be sure. I briefly scanned the wood-paneled walls crammed with photos of sports teams and plaques honouring Lee Donison; there was also a large framed photo of a house nearly hidden behind trees. The room was outfitted sparsely with a treatment table, a couple of metal filing cabinets, and an old wooden desk with two rolling office chairs. Lee politely invited me to take his armchair for our interview, while he took the patient's chair.

"Lee," I began, once the tape recorder was running, "have you always been a healer?"

"Well, I worked for 37 years in the insurance business," he replied, mildly. "And before that, I was a cook and a butcher. But I've been doing this . . . well, since the '50s anyways."

"And when did you realize you were a healer?" I asked.

"Oh my goodness," he said, frowning slightly with the strain of remembering something long ago. "When I was at the farm. I was born and raised on a farm. And I'd work on my mother's headaches – she was in a car accident – I'd work on her shoulders, her arms, her back . . . ."

"But were other people in your family doing that?" I said. "I mean, how did you learn?"

"My father was a self-taught veterinarian, that's all." Lee smiled, bashfully. "So I don't know whether I have any of his ability or not, but it just always came to me. And then, about 1961 or '62, I met a world-famous psychic by chance, here in Regina. He was Little Louie, from Little Louie and the Rascals. Anyway, I'd been doing some healing before then and I was talked into going to listen to his lecture – there were about 15 or 20 of us that went together. After the lecture was over, a lady asked him if he could look around the room and see anything about any particular individual. So he looked right at me and he said, 'That man is a healer; he can restore eyesight, he can take headaches away, he can fix limbs and muscles,' and so on. Everybody looked, and then I was ready to crawl under the table – or the chairs, rather – I was embarrassed," Lee said, chuckling softly. "And he said, 'I want to talk to you after the show.'

So afterwards he told me I have to do it or I wouldn't live very long."

"You have to do it?" I said, now hooked. "What did he mean you won't live very long?"

"He told me, 'If you don't do it, that energy you have is going to burn you out,'" Lee answered matter-of-factly. "He said I have to use what I've been given to use. Since then, it's just like the floodgates were opened. That was about '61 or '62."

I was starting to notice some qualities which would have made Lee a great fighter. For one, he was quick and decisive in his answers. He did not fidget or shift around in his chair. He was completely focused on the moment, undisturbed by the ringing telephone or the new voices out in the hall. But mostly, it was his intensity. His dark brown eyes were fixed on me the whole time without seemingly blinking; I couldn't get out of his range. This created a very firm yet impassive connection.

I asked him what conditions he'd healed over the years, what diseases he had cured. But he bobbed and weaved, too humble to list off his accomplishments.

"Well," I said, probing further, "someone told me that one time a wrestler was in a competition and he sprained his ankle and couldn't go back out, and that you were there and put your hands on his ankle and a couple minutes later he was healed." I had him in the corner.

"Yes, that's right," said Lee. "He went back and competed. It was a provincial championship meet."

"And you can do that?" I prompted him. "Heal an injury, within minutes?"

"Oh yes. I don't care how badly an ankle is sprained, I usually can repair it and tape it and they go back out and play. I've had football players, hockey players come in – I do a lot of the Weyburn Redwings as you see there (he turned to point to a framed and signed team photo on a wall) and Humboldt Broncos, Notre Dame Hounds, Melville Millionaires, the Riders, the Rams . . . ."

Lee readily admitted he had no medical training, he had studied no texts. He referred only to a well-worn medical picturebook that his wife had found in the Golden Mile Shopping Centre 'grab-box.' Rather, he said, he can simply see the injury internally.

"Really!" I blurted. "Well how do you see it, do you see the actual body parts?"

"Yes, I see the injury as it is; therefore, I just have to reverse it. It's difficult to say how I see it, but it's like a *knowing*. It's just like, if you've ever played sports, you can anticipate something – where the puck is going to go, where the ball is going to go – and you go for it before it lands, before the pass comes there you intercept it. It's almost the same way."

We both looked around the walls, at the medley of framed sports photos, and I commented on the collages of Thank You cards.

"Oh goodness," Lee said, smiling, "I've got several hundred cards from people that have written me afterwards and thanked me. I used to throw them away, and then my kids gave me heck, they said, 'Why don't you save them, Dad!' So I've got them up on the wall, and in the drawer there, a bunch of them." He now noticed an envelope on the desk. Reaching for it, he said, "And this is just one of the things that I've done if you want to read that."

I pulled out the card and a photo of a chubby, laughing baby fell out. I read aloud: "Our baby Alexandra was born with a life-threatening condition called a congenital diaphragmatic hernia. A hole in her diaphragm caused her stomach, pancreas, spleen and intestines to push up through into her chest activity, causing her heart to shift to the right and her left lung to stop growing. As a result, her esophagus was constricted and she did not have the ability to swallow. After a major surgery at six days old, she remained on a ventilator for one month and in the ICU for two months. She was fed through a tube through her nose. The common problem with most babies born with CDH is that they do not eat very well and lose weight. After months of consulting many medical professionals, my mom suggested that I phone Lee Donison. He agreed to see us right away. In a matter of days, I noticed a slight improvement with her eating and after seven treatments there was marked improvement. She is now eight months old and eats without any problem at all. Her doctors are skeptical. However, I attribute this to the healing nature of Lee Donison."

I looked up from the card, curious about something. "Lee, aren't you afraid about the doctors or hospitals saying you're not licensed?"

"Well, the doctors were skeptical when the parents took that baby out of the hospital to bring her here. But if they would have left her in the hospital, I would have gone to see her there, too. I have gone up many times to the hospital and worked on people. The nurses mostly know me, the doctors know me, they don't say anything."

"But how do you protect yourself, in the eyes of the law?"

"I don't," he sighed, in resignation. "I can't even *get* insurance because I'm not a professional. I suspect that if I tried now, I could, but I'm so close to maybe retiring that I say, 'Why bother?' But I'm pretty careful; if someone comes in, and my antennae go up, I just give them a light massage and tell them I can't help them."

His eyes studied mine for my next move. I asked him if he could heal himself, too.

"I have, yes. Because I've gone several times to therapists, chiropractors, and I wasn't happy with what they were doing. It's a simple thing once you've had the injury yourself and you *have* to correct it, then you know how to do it for others."

"So have you had a lot of these injuries?"

"Oh yes, being in the sports I was in, I had a lot of injuries. Ankles, knees, backs, ribs. There's a rib thing that the doctors operate on, where your floating rib folds underneath the body like this," and he demonstrated by pushing his lowest rib in. "And it locks there and it heals that way, and you can't even breathe. So they have to operate to release it. I can release it," he said snapping his fingers, "takes about two minutes. All these things are simple, if you do them right."

I nodded, hoping for more.

"Or sacroiliac is a back problem, it's just in here," he said turning and pointing to his lower back. "So many people have that problem. It twists the spine, and again they operate on the spine. But it's really just a five-minute adjustment for the hip. Painless, totally painless. I had a doctor come in here, he said his patients found it went away after they came here. He'd lifted his boat and twisted himself. So he came, it was fixed in minutes and he couldn't believe it."

"So you do have doctors who believe in you?"

"Oh yes. I had an orthopedic surgeon who brought his wife here. I worked on her knees, she was much better, and he said, 'You know, Lee, I *operate* on knees like that, how do you do it?'"

I met his unfaltering gaze. "And how do you do it?" I implored him.

He ducked in diffidence. "Oh goodness, I don't know," he said. "It just comes to me whenever I put my hands on someone. Now it's gotten to the point that I can even tell on the telephone where their problem is and how to repair it."

"Without even seeing them?" I asked, a mix of admiration and skepticism.

Lee was solid, unphased. "Yes, long distance healing, I've done that a fair bit, where people phone from a great distance and I'll say, 'Well just sit back and relax at a certain time – I'll tell them a certain time – and call me back in an hour or two if the pain is still there,' and they'll call me back and the pain is gone. But anyway, if someone phones and says that they have a headache, or their ribs are sore or their knee is sore, I'll know exactly how it is and quite often I tell them how they hurt themselves. And they'll say, 'Oh, right, I forgot all about that!' It's just something . . . I never even think about this anymore." He shrugged offhandedly, as if it really was nothing.

A couple of years previous, I'd heard a fascinating story about long-distance healing in which a young B.C. healer named Adam cured the legendary musician Ronnie Hawkins of terminal pancreatic cancer – from 3,000 miles away. In 2002, Hawkins was told by his surgeons that he had an inoperable tumour and was given six months to live. Sixteen-year-old Adam contacted Hawkins and offered to help. For three weeks, at the same time every night (allowing for time zone differences), Adam in Vancouver and Hawkins in Peterborough would sit quietly for a few minutes. Adam would look at a photo of Hawkins until he felt a jolt; meanwhile, Hawkins reported he'd feel a tingling sensation. At that point, Adam would be able to visualize the tumour and bombard it with light energy. After several sessions, Adam told Hawkins he could see that the cancer had died and the mass was dissipating. Months later, Hawkins had a CT scan and MRI; both confirmed the cancerous tumour was gone.

Now Lee told me about a recent incident, in which a woman from Port Arthur phoned. She was having intense pain in her shoulder, so he spent 20 minutes sending her healing energy. Afterward she phoned him, saying she had seen white light coming down for those 20 minutes, then her arm suddenly shot out and there was no more pain.

"And is that what you visualize – a white light – for healing?" I'd heard of the white light; I was back on my toes.

"Yes, yes," he said, nodding. "This is a form of energy. That's all. Restoring eyesight is just using energy. All I do is I put a Kleenex over the person's eyes, and I place my hands above the Kleenex, and they can see. I had a lady, her husband had to lead her in. I was standing right here at the door, she couldn't even see me. But she walked back out on her own."

I must have looked a little punch-drunk.

"No, really," he said, emphatically. "People come in, they have to be led in, they can't see anything. They go out crying, because they can see. Same with hearing, headaches . . . I'm embarrassed to even talk about it." He smiled modestly, shook his head.

"What about arthritis?" I asked, getting an idea. "Have you healed that?"

"Oh yes. I'm working on one lady now with arthritis, she has to come regularly. She couldn't even walk, she was in a wheelchair the first few times she came here. She was very, very bad – she couldn't open the door because her fingers were so gnarled up. Now she's driving her own vehicle, she's walking. Sometimes with a cane, but most of the time without a cane."

I scribbled down a reminder to myself to follow up on this. "So Lee, do you call yourself a healer?"

"No, I just call myself Lee." He laughed. "No, but others . . . do."

"Are you religious?" I asked him.

"Well, I say a prayer before I touch anyone. I ask for God's guidance and assistance. And I know it's not me that does it, it's done through me."

"What are more of the memorable times that you've helped people?"

He shrugged his shoulders, not comfortable with talking about himself like this. I also got the impression that he really didn't want to sell this to me; it made no difference to him whether I believed what he was telling me or not. For him, it was simply the way it is. But he was not in the habit of proselytizing to others.

"Well," he offered reticently, "this lady that just left here when you were coming in, she had tumours on the breast, one was malignant. And the last test she had, it was gone."

"And she didn't do anything else except come to you?"

"That's right. This Friday, she's going for another scan. Just to make sure, the doctor said every month she's going to have a scan. But they said the last two scans showed nothing."

He told me it takes two or three treatments to fix most problems.

"Do you take care of yourself, Lee? To keep your energy up – do you eat healthily?"

He said that he didn't smoke or drink, and that he tried to keep a balanced lifestyle and diet. "I used to jog three miles a day too, with my jogging partners," he said, a little wistful, and I could sense there was some pain behind this story. "And they both passed on with non-Hodgkins lymphoma, both the same thing. We used to run three to five miles a day. But after that I thought, well they both ran the same place, they both got non-Hodgkins lymphoma – in the groin and the gland here – and I got paranoid so I quit running." He laughed, embarrassed at this admission.

"Could you have worked on their non-Hodgkins lymphoma, can you work on things like that?"

Lee paused before answering. There was sorrow in his voice when he did. "You know, they never asked me. At that time, I wasn't working on cancer and they never asked me. And I will never ask somebody to work on them, they have to ask for help. My feeling is this: if you ask for help, you're ready for it. If you don't ask for help, I probably won't help you very much. I don't say, 'Well let me look at the problem . . . .' I used to when I first started, and I found it was too hard. People didn't know what I was doing, they didn't believe that I could do it, and it was too difficult."

I'd been told that Lee is busy healing people from eight o'clock in the morning until late evening, most days of the week.

"Yes, my wife is trying to cut me down a little bit," he said, sheepishly. "Especially in tournament season, I don't get finished 'til near midnight many times. But normally, I see anywhere from 25 to 35 people a day. As long as I'm here, that phone rings constantly."

I'd noticed; the shrill ring had jarred me several times by this point. I asked him when he would finally hang up the gloves.

"As long as God tells me I can still do it, I'll do it. If I am able to work on bodies, I guess I'll do it. I've tried to retire a couple of times, but after many phone calls and people saying, 'Oh please, just see me,' and 'Just me,' and 'Just me,' where do you stop?"

"Well, do you think you can teach this to somebody? Could you mentor someone?"

"I've tried – at least three, four people – but I haven't found anyone good enough that I have confidence in sending all of my patients to. They'd have to have some knowledge of the anatomy . . . and it really depends what their intentions are. If their purpose in life is to help someone, then they're coming from the right direction, they have the right things in mind. But if they're thinking of making lots of money, then I don't even bother."

"And do you charge a certain amount for your services, Lee?"

"Whatever people can pay." He shrugged. "I have a box there," he said, pointing to a wooden box with a slit in the top, sitting on a cabinet, "and they just put in what they want. Now this morning I had, I think, six people in here." He walked over to the cabinet, opened the box, chuckled, then walked back and showed me the contents: two toonies and a pair of earrings. "Anyway, whatever they can afford is fine – oh, I'm sorry and somebody gave me this, this morning." He produced a $20 bill from his pants pocket. Then he sat down in the chair again.

"So how do you feel about your life being so much taken up by this?"

"I'm fortunate that I have a wonderful wife. She understands the situation, and that's the reason I can still do it. I would love to have more free time. We have an acreage – we have a quarter-section, that's our place out there," he said pointing to the photo on the wall of the house behind trees. "We built everything there, and we run out there and hide when we want some respite, some quiet. The deer come into the yard there and play." He grinned with that sentimental disclosure.

I heard someone come in the front door. "Oh, do you have an appointment at noon, Lee?"

"Yes I do," he said, now serious. His voice dropped a little, in respect. "This fellow here has MS. Again, he couldn't walk when he came in, he was brought in in a wheelchair. And he's walking now, he's functioning almost normally."

I gathered up my things, thanked Lee profusely for sharing his time with me, and walked out of the treatment room. As I was putting on my shoes in the hall, a tall man in his 40s eagerly walked up to greet Lee and entered the treatment room. This healthy-looking guy was recently beaten down by degenerative, incurable Multiple Sclerosis?

Knockout!

* * *

Now I see Joyce's car coming up the crescent. I wave to her and she motions that she'll find a place to park. I hope Lee is able to help her. After that interview with him in August, I had arrived at her house breathless with anecdotes of Lee Donison and his healing hands. And, I'd stated most pointedly, he's had some success working on arthritis. Right then and there, Greg phoned and arranged for his mother to see Lee about her debilitating arthritis. The soonest Lee could see her was in early January: today.

Last week I had phoned Joyce and asked if I could accompany her to see Lee. She had hedged a little; if the truth be told, she wasn't sure she was going to keep this appointment. No specialists or therapists had been able to do much about an ankle that had been causing her such grief for 15 years now – she was skeptical that this folk healer could do anything for her. However, with Greg regularly prodding her about her pending appointment, and now me wanting to come with her to observe Lee Donison in action, she was slightly hemmed in.

"Good morning, Joyce!" I greet her.

"Hello Jacquie, nice to see you," she says, smiling. "How was your drive down this morning?" Her face is full of expression and life, but her body is incompliant as she limps up to the house. Her frustration and pain are evident as she awkwardly climbs the steps. "This *damn* ankle!" she growls.

We ring the doorbell; after some moments, Lee answers and invites us in. "Mr. Donison?" asks Joyce, by way of introducing herself.

"No," is his flat reply.

"Oh," says Joyce, slightly confused.

I wince in this awkwardness.

"You're not Mr. Donison?" she tries again.

"No," he repeats. "I'm Lee."

Joyce relaxes in response to his gesture of informality. "Okay . . . *Lee*," she says.

Now more confusion; apparently Lee wasn't expecting her until tomorrow morning. Joyce says her son made the appointment for her months ago, and has been reminding her repeatedly that she's booked for this morning at 9:30; Lee says there's always a mix-up when other people make appointments for someone else, and a person should always make their own appointments. Joyce states that, regardless of who made the mistake, it's too bad that I have driven all the way from Saskatoon this morning for nothing. So Lee says he will try to squeeze her in before noon.

Joyce and I sit in the living room to wait, and spend the time chatting about our recent Christmas holidays. Several times, the front door opens;

several times I hear Lee walking people out of the treatment room and bidding them good-bye. Eventually he peers around the corner and invites us to follow him into his room.

"Okay, sit in the recliner here," says Lee. As Joyce hobbles over to the chair, she asks him if he once worked in insurance; she says her husband recognized his name as a colleague in the business. Lee says yes, he worked in insurance. "That was a hundred years ago," he says. He shows her how to recline the chair, then pulls a stool over and sits on it, facing her raised feet. "Now what is that limp about?"

I lean up against the desk as Joyce explains that she'd broken her right ankle in 1978, and the surgeon had repaired it using screws. However, 12 years later it was causing her pain, so the screws were removed. "But arthritis has set in there, and it has done nothing but give me grief ever since," she says.

Lee places his hands on her swollen, misshapen ankle. "Okay, relax it now," he says. "Where does it hurt? When you do this?" He gently moves the ankle back and forth.

"All over, yes," says Joyce. "I have very little movement."

He frowns as his fingers probe around her ankle. "The bones are not lined up right," says Lee. "You know that, hey?"

"Well it wasn't until about 15 years ago it started bothering me," says Joyce.

"Um-hm, and that's arthritis," says Lee. "The ankle gets weaker, you get older, the bones lose their elasticity, you lose some of the cartilage between each bone, it gets softer and softer and then it starts to shift. That's what happens. And when you're walking on it, you're wearing out the whole mechanism in your ankle. So what we have to do is line that up again, until the ankle is tracking normally and straight. Right now it's not tracking normally."

"Oh yeah," says Joyce, "and sometimes . . . ."

"It hurts like crazy," Lee says.

"I can hardly walk . . . ," Joyce continues.

"Well, sure," agrees Lee.

"Because it's just a wreck."

Lee frowns and shakes his head as he palpates her ankle. "The bones are all out of alignment," he states, deadpan, "and you're going to crush all these bones in here and then they'll have to cut it off here and you'll need a whole new ankle, a new foot."

Joyce looks surprised, then laughs. "Yes, well that's what I would opt for! If you lived with this, you'd be glad to have it lopped off." She rolls her eyes in exasperation.

"Well, let's fix it instead," says Lee gently. "You still have an appointment tomorrow, and I'll have time then to put the heat on here and soften this up. Then we'll be able to work it, because this is all scar tissue back here. We'll put hot wet towels on it and break up that scar tissue. You know when you have a tough roast, you put it in the pot and boil it. What happens?"

Joyce grins. "It gets pretty tender," she says.

"Exactly, and that's what we'll do," says Lee. He is distractedly looking at the floor on his left side as he manipulates her ankle, feeling the situation. "Okay," he says, turning to focus on Joyce, "you've got to relax, you've got to let me work it. Every time I touch it, you're pulling your ankle back and forth. I can't do anything. You ever try to thread a needle when somebody's hitting your elbow?"

We all laugh. The atmosphere is now relaxed, positive.

"There, let it go," he encourages her, looking off to his side again. "Let it go. It's just out of alignment, it's way out of alignment. Let it go." He turns to her. "Is it hurting?"

"Yes," Joyce concedes. "But that's okay, it hurts anyway. I guess I've just lived with it so long, Lee, that I expect it to be sore."

"No," Lee declares. "No, you don't expect anything to be sore. Expect it to be fit. As a fiddle. I'm going to . . . ," and his hands make a synchronized movement around her ankle, "okay, just about got it. Let it go, let it go. It's got to go a little bit more, that's all." His hands rotate quickly. "There, did you feel that?"

"I felt *that* one!" says Joyce.

"Okay, I'll just show you what's happening," says Lee, and he stands up and rummages across the desktop. "Where's my book? I'll show you what an ankle looks like." He leafs through his dog-eared medical picturebook, then stops at a page; Joyce and I both lean in to look. "There, you see how many bones are in that ankle? Just get one that's not tracking right, and it'll throw everything off."

"Yes," says Joyce, "and of course I went to Dr. (so-and-so, an orthopedic surgeon) . . . ."

"Oh, well," says Lee flatly, "you might as well have gone to the grocery store." I chuckle at Lee's simple candour. He places the book back on the desk, and sits down to work her ankle some more.

"I tell you," says Joyce, "I was really disappointed in him. I went to him and he says, 'Well, you've got two choices: you can live with it or we can fuse it.'"

Lee laughs loudly, as if that was a punchline.

Joyce says, "And I thought, 'Cripe! I waited ten months to see this guy and that's what he tells me?'" She rolls her eyes. "Oh! I just felt *that*. It went 'click'."

"Okay," says Lee. "Take it up and down now, is it sore?"

Joyce moves her foot around. "Not as much," she says, shaking her head.

"Okay, set your foot down on the ground. Is it sore?"

She slides her foot off the rest, and places it on the floor. "It's stiff," she says.

"Yeah, but is it painful?"

"No," says Joyce, and looks over to me, raising her eyebrows in surprise.

"Now I'm going to set this," says Lee, lifting her foot up again to work on it, "and then I'm going to tape it for you, and then you'll have to come here probably 150 times." Joyce and I giggle; there is now a giddy air of optimism in the room. "No," he smiles, "probably one, maybe two more times." He wraps white sports tape around her ankle with deftness and speed. "There."

"Oh yeah!" exclaims Joyce, standing up from the chair. "That's much better, Lee!"

"I'm going to put the heat on it tomorrow for about 20 minutes, half an hour," says Lee. "I have to realign all the bones in there. But you'll see, there'll be virtually no pain."

Joyce snorts in disbelief. "And I've lived with this for all my life? Well it *feels* like all my life. If you could know how I have suffered with this damn thing."

"How does it feel now, walking on it?" Lee asks.

"Well it doesn't hurt as much," says Joyce, shaking her head in wonder. "I can still feel it a little bit, but my God, I've been walking on it like that for 15 years!"

"So what I did," says Lee, "is to shift it over. Now you'll have to get used to walking in this new position."

"That's fine Lee, whatever it takes," says Joyce, clearly marveling at this new sensation of walking without pain. And then remembering something that had not yet been dealt with, she says, "Okay, do I pay you now?"

"No," says Lee.

"Oh . . . ," says Joyce, uncertainly. Then, with renewed confidence: "Right, I can pay you when I come tomorrow."

"No," says Lee, firmly. "You don't pay until the ankle is fixed."

And at that point, I see there are tears in Joyce's eyes. No one has ever given her this much hope.

* * *

Two weeks later, I call Joyce; she has now seen Lee three times. "So is your ankle any better?" I ask her.

"Oh yes, completely!" She is avid. "I'm walking without limping. Isn't that remarkable? I can't believe it!"

Joyce tells me she recently walked two full rounds at a local indoor track, something she has not been able to do for 15 years. She says Lee is going to work a little on her left knee which has been thrown out over time by the limp – and then she thinks she'll even be able to swing a golf club again this summer.

My friend Greg confirms the good news when I talk to him. "Oh, she's completely blown away by the improvement," he says. "It's definitely the best thing that's happened to her in regards to that issue. Her only regret was that she didn't go to see Lee ten years ago." He tells me his mother is very grateful to have met Lee.

As I hang up the phone, I think: *Me, too.*

I'm grateful to have met this wonderfully paradoxical person: a small and gentle fellow who is in the Sports Hall of Fame as one of the best fighters in the country; a modest man with no medical training who quietly treats all manner of disease with simple focused energy while governments and pharmaceutical companies spend billions of dollars trying to get the same results; an insurance agent who can't get insurance.

God love him.

INTO THE MYSTIC

"If the doors of perception were cleansed every thing would appear to man as it is, infinite. For man has closed himself up, till he sees all things thro' narrow chinks of his cavern."

From *The Marriage of Heaven and Hell*, William Blake

I was 15 when I went for a two-week course to the Saskatchewan School of the Arts, or Fort San, as it was known. I had no idea of the history of that place, had no further thought than to craft one good story under the tutelage of my writing instructor, David Carpenter. The cerebrally demanding class, coupled with the fresh air at that Qu'Appelle Valley estate, made for deep and long nighttime slumbers. On my third night there however, I was pulled awake by the sensation of someone watching me sleep.

Opening my eyes, I saw a woman sitting in a chair beside my bed facing me. She was in her late teens or early 20s, she had long, straight blond hair, and she was wearing a white nightgown. She stared at me with no discernible expression on her face. In that moment, my rational mind determined this must be Cathy G., a classmate whose dorm room was just down the hall. Bleary-eyed, I said, "Cathy, what are you doing?" She peered back at me but didn't answer. Now becoming concerned, I demanded, "Cathy, are you okay?" She said nothing. By then fully alert, I sat up and turned on the overhead reading light. She was gone.

Only later did I find out that Fort San had been a tuberculosis sanatorium from 1917 to 1972, that hundreds of people had died there, that there was still a crematorium on the grounds. And only by chance did I discover that the woman watching me sleep had been seen by many others staying in this same building (the West Wing of the main residence) over the years. In fact, one witness was so affected by this specter that she did some research and concluded the young woman's name had been Alice, and that she had died of TB many years ago at Fort San.

Alice opened up a significant new area in my life: she provided me with proof of a spirit realm. Proof of a dimension not understood – or even acknowledged – by mainstream science, but nonetheless well-documented throughout human history.

In life, I do feel it's important to accept what is shown to you, even though it may be disturbing or nonsensical. My aim is to be benignly receptive, and to remain open to possibilities. Since that incident with Alice, I have had several other illuminating experiences which allowed my perception of reality to expand. These revelations always unfolded through happenstance . . . or maybe it wasn't chance at all, but a perfectly timed series of serendipitous events.

And so it was that in the spring of 2005, I happened to pop in briefly at an old colleague's place, just as he was having a quick coffee with an out-of-town visitor en route to Germany, who casually mentioned to me that there's a Métis woman named Rose Richardson up at Green Lake who has an extraordinary knowledge of medicinal plants – and that this information comes to her in dreams and visions. He gave me the phone number of the Keewatin Junction Station, the Métis museum and café that Rose and her husband Ric own.

I phoned the Keewatin Station, and explained to Ric that I was writing a book on Saskatchewan folk healers, and that I'd heard about Rose and would very much like to meet her. Ric told me to come by anytime. "We're closed Mondays," he said, "but otherwise we're always here."

When the day came for me to drive to Green Lake, I was feeling worn out. My husband and I had been hosting a work-bee at our cabin in the woods near Big River that whole week, and I was tender with sunburn, irritated by bug-bites, and disheartened by the magnitude of the building project. Plus I was tired – we were hauling wood and hammering nails from sun-up 'til sundown every day. Still, it was only an hour from our cabin to Green Lake; it made sense to go meet Rose while I was up in the area.

Keewatin Junction, I soon discovered, is a historical CPR railway station originally from Meadow Lake, and now the steward of the corner where Highways 55 and 155 meet. The building was set back from the asphalt, with an expanse of tended green grass in front of it, and the wild forest behind it. In traditional red paint and white trim, the station had a front deck sporting a white 'Railway Crossing' sign, and several Canadian flags waving along the railing. From the second-storey dormer, two large Métis Nation flags, one red and one blue, danced in the wind. In the back, old wagon wheels leaned against the wood siding, and a life-sized eagle carved of stone was the mute custodian of the steps leading up to the café entrance.

The screen door creaked open; I stepped inside to a visual and olfactory feast. Wide plank flooring led past the open kitchen and counter on the right, into a room of ten or so chunky wooden tables with solid wooden chairs. The golden, fir-paneled walls hosted a gallery of black and white photos, along with antique saw-blades and drying herbs. The aromas of homemade soup, bannock, and pie infused the space and were most welcoming – as was the smiling and gracious Ric, who walked up to greet me. He was in his late 40s, wearing a black button-up shirt, blue jeans ornamented with a bearclaw belt buckle, and an elaborate bracelet of carved mammoth ivory around his wrist. With his shoulder-length wavy locks, and silver horseshoe-shaped beard, he could have been cast as a character from the American Wild West in the 1800s. He was an enthusiastic and engaging host, offering me a coffee at the 'Help Yourself' coffee bar, and then showing me around the café to introduce me to some of the Métis people in the framed photos: Elders, political figures and war veterans – many of them his or Rose's ancestors.

Rose appeared from the kitchen and quietly shook my hand. Also in her late 40s, she was wearing a burgundy apron over a black t-shirt and black jeans. I was impressed by her powerful presence, even though (I later realized) she was actually much smaller than I. Her long, dark, thick hair framed her aristocratic cheekbones and regal jaw. She had large black eyes that maintained a polite distance by only meeting mine every so often; but when they did, it was with a deep and discerning calmness.

Rose left the room briefly and returned with a round drum to perform, she said, a welcome song for me. She held the drum in her left hand, and used a felt-tipped stick to tap it with her right hand. "Warming it up," she explained, as she listened for a new tone in the taut skin. "The drum is like a heartbeat," she said over the rhythmic beat: *da-dum, da-dum, da-dum.* "You welcome the people that come," *da-dum, da-dum, da-dum,* "but you also welcome the spirits." And then she sang, in low-toned vibrato, a two-verse song in her native tongue. I was honoured and thrilled by this unexpected gesture. The song ended with a strong flourish of steady beating: *dum-dum-dum-dum-dum-dum-dum.* The tone was set; everyone was here.

We three helped ourselves at the coffee bar, then sat at a table together and allowed the conversation to find its path. Rose was completely present in a quiet way, while Ric was talkative and articulate. He had a lot to say about Métis history, Métis politics, the Métis culture. It was Rose and Ric's passion for their Métis heritage that inspired them to create this restaurant and cultural museum. In the early '90s, Rose had bought the old railway station she remembered so well from her childhood days in Meadow Lake and had moved it an hour's drive east to its home today. They had spent two full years restoring the old building, and then spent the last four years trying to make a viable living from it.

"It's our wish for Keewatin Junction to become a self-sustaining centre of learning," said Ric. "Where Métis people can come for workshops, social gatherings, cultural events – and where people from other cultures would be able to share their traditional teachings with us as well," he said. "Because aboriginal teachings are based on the Medicine

Wheel, which has four directions and actually encompasses four races of people."

"Yes," Rose now entered the conversation. "That's my dream and my vision, for people from all over the world, from the four directions, to come together to share and to make good medicine. And if they say, 'Okay, let's put our heart medicine together instead of competing over whose is better,' and the Creator joined with us, then the medicine would be powerful and good for everybody."

At this point, two men came into the restaurant, and Rose left our table to get them some soup and bannock. "Here, I'll show you the museum," Ric said, standing up. "Come with me." So I followed him into the back portion of the building where there was a birchbark canoe on display, along with buffalo skulls and robes, and a Great Horned Owl preserved in pursuit of a Spruce Hen. A glass showcase housed aboriginal beadwork and leatherwork, as well as Ric's carved moose antler jewelry and mammoth tusk sculptures.

One wall featured a couple dozen local plants pressed and labeled behind glass frames; these were some of the treasures to be found on the Medicine Walks that Rose and Ric facilitate. Ric told me they host these walks to educate people on the powerful remedies underfoot, and to teach them sustained and respectful usage of the plants. "There are some real blessings that have been placed on the ground by the Creator," said Ric, "in the form of these plants that grow wherever the diseases are, so that they can help us."

I was awed to also see a framed, full-page newspaper story on Rose and Ric – as special guests at the Chelsea Flower Show in London, May of 2005. Having grown up with a mother, grandmother and several aunts who cannot walk past any flower, bush or tree without giving its Latin name and common name and preferred growing conditions, I already knew that the annual Chelsea Flower Show is a premiere event in the world for horticulturists.

"Rose and I were invited to be interpretive guides there, at the first-ever boreal forest display," Ric said, politely poised. The living exhibit had included a central pond surrounded by many different species of trees, mosses and plants. Rose and Ric had explained the unique Canadian ecosystem to the thousands of visitors that came through that week – visitors that included Ringo Starr, the Duke of York, and Rod Stewart. Their display won the silver medal in the Show Garden category.

At the request of Taiga Rescue Network, Rose and Ric were in Chelsea to educate the public on sustainable use of the boreal forest, and to promote 'non-timber forest products.' "NTFPs include teas, foods, traditional medicines and certain handicrafts such as moose-antler carvings," said Ric. "Anything that the forest produces, except for wood." He added that he and Rose aren't against the timber companies in general. "Just those that practice unsustainable exploitation of the woods."

We walked back into the café, and sat again at our table. Rose joined us; I sensed she wanted to talk now. I mentioned to her how I'd learned of her, that I was told she is a healer who has visions.

She smiled at me, then said in a slow, thoughtful way, "Personally, I'm not quite sure if I consider myself to be a 'healer.' I work with a lot of people, but . . . I'm not powerful enough to say that I can call the spirits and call the Creator anytime I want. And there's nobody that *is* that powerful." Her voice got softer. "So I'm leery about people acting as if they possess all kinds of magic. Because if I had that type of magic, maybe I'd be a magician instead."

We both laughed. It was the first of many moments I enjoyed Rose's gentle sense of humour.

But, she affirmed in a staid manner, the spirits do let her know what's happening; such as when someone sick may be coming to see her. "If someone's going to come over to visit tomorrow, if it's meant to be I will know about it beforehand. And I will know about it not through fax, email or telephone. I'll just know about it and prepare for it. It's almost like a force that draws you into doing something."

The restaurant door opened and three highway workers in bright orange coveralls sat down at a table. Ric got up, then walked over to them with a coffee carafe in hand. Soon the four of them were in an animated conversation about the Department of Highways.

Rose looked back to me. "I usually hold back with people at first and let the spirits tell me it's okay, you know. I take direction from them," she said. "And they let me know with each person. Like when you first came, I didn't say much because I had to get the spirits to check you out first and then they said it was okay, and then it was okay with me."

This was encouraging; I felt I could now interview her. So I asked her how she knows which plants to use for healing, and again, she said the spirits guide her. They always had, she said, ever since she could remember. "When I was a little girl, the Elders would come and 'borrow' me from my mother. They'd say, 'Can we borrow your girl for a little while to show us where the medicine grows?' And I'd leave with the Elders, and we'd walk along in the forest and when my body would tingle, then I'd know the medicine was there. But I'd say, 'Don't pick this plant, it's just the pointer, it's telling us that the medicine is here.' I don't know where I got all that information about the plant being the pointer, but then I'd show them where the *right* plants were. And then I'd go off to play. I'd climb trees until all of a sudden I'd know it was time to leave and I'd go to the Elders and I'd say, 'That's it, we have to stop now and go home,' and they'd stop, and we'd walk home."

However, she said, that only worked when the plants were appropriate for those particular people. "You know, there were some people I could take year after year and the plants would not show, even though we would walk and walk. And then I'd know that it was not intended that I show these people where the plants were. So I'd say, 'Okay, they grew here before but they're not here anymore.' And they'd get really upset, and we'd go home. But I'd go back out on my own about an hour later and the plants would all be there. You know it was okay, but I just took the wrong people. So it's not always that the plants will appear."

However, said Rose, most people don't understand that. She told me of an example, when she and Ric had been invited to participate at the First Nation International Healing and Medicines Gathering held at Neekaneet First Nation in 2000. They set up their teepee on the grounds and were available during the gathering for ailing people to come to them for help. "There were people waiting outside, you know, people that were having problems and wanted to see me. And this one lady would come early in the morning and she'd sit in my teepee, and she'd ask all kinds of questions. 'What is this plant used for, what is this plant used for,' and she had a little book and she was just filling that book up. And finally I told her, 'I appreciate you coming here, I don't mind you coming here, but you're doing a lot of writing. And it's not for anything specific, it's not for somebody that you love and you want to help them. You want to come here and get all you can out of me and write it so you'll remember, because you want to do that yourself. But you know,' I said, 'by the time you leave this ground you won't even have your papers. Because it's not intended; the spirits will take it back.' And I knew that the spirits were not happy about her coming in and being like a psychic vampire, just trying to draw as much as she could from the people. So I told her, 'If you have a specific interest about somebody that you love very much who's really sick, then you'll have that. But that's all you're going to remember. And you're not going to have your papers.'"

Ric had quietly joined our table again. He was nodding now, smiling. He added, "And it was true. She'd lost her notebook by the end of the gathering. She took away nothing anyway." His expression turned serious. "But she wasn't ill. I think she was trying to write a book – and this was not the right place for it. People were coming there who needed help, and this reporter was taking away from the time that Rose could spend with those people."

I nodded in understanding. Then for a stricken instant, I wondered if I, too, was taking Rose away from more important matters. But there didn't seem to be anything else she wanted to be doing; she looked relaxed and contented to be sitting here, talking.

"Rose, what about the dreams and visions?" I asked her. "What are they like?"

"Sometimes it can be just a message in my mind," answered Rose. "And I just have to have faith, I have to take time to *listen*. And that's why a lot of times I need my own quiet time. You know, some people spend a lot of time praying, but when they're finished, they're finished. I mean, they never take the time to listen. And I think that is a problem with our society today; we get messages, but we don't hear them."

"Yes," said Ric. "These days praying is just instant gratification. People are asking for what they want, instead of asking for direction or guidance. And sometimes it takes time, you know. God's not your servant. Even when you pray."

Usually, Rose said, she prays and then she listens for the messages to come to her. Sometimes it happens when she's sleeping, sometimes while she's busy doing something. "And it's not like a voice that says, *'Rose, use nettle this time',*" she said in an exaggerated deep voice. Her dark eyes crinkled up in a warm smile. "You know, it's not anything like that. But it's from somewhere," she said, looking off to the distance. "It's from somewhere. I get direction."

She focused on me again. "Like when I first met Ric, he had problems with his knees," said Rose. "I mean our house is 60 feet long, and whenever he'd get up or come walking, I'd hear his knees cracking from a long way off. And so I prayed, I asked for direction, I said, 'What can I do?'" Her voice softened with emotion. "You know, 'What can I *do*?' And my instructions came in terms of, you mix the bear grease, you add this herb and then this one. So I did, and he hasn't had that problem since. And now that medicine is kind of like a base we use for lots of things."

Ric said that many people, even Medicine People, come to learn from Rose. "And they want to know who taught her," he said, "who her teacher was. In Indian culture, this kind of knowledge is a gift, which is passed on to the grandchildren. And we feel that a lot of it is actually genetic memory."

About then, I noticed that my previous lethargy had transformed into exhilaration. I was feeling so damn lucky to be in the presence of these two. Rose was like a fantastic iceberg to me. What I could see of her was wondrous, but I strongly sensed there was a depth and magnitude that was 'under water.' In a whole other element.

At this point, an older fellow walked into the restaurant; clearly a regular here, he helped himself to a coffee. Ric filled up his own coffee mug and then joined this newcomer at a table a few down from ours. Rose smiled at the men, then with a trailing smile she looked back to me, and began telling me about a recent incident where a couple stopped in at the café on their drive back to Edmonton. Rose said she could see they were both in a lot of pain, and found out they were recovering from a rollover accident. So she invited first the woman, and then the man, into a back room where she rubbed specific medicines on their injuries. "And then when they were going to leave, I gave them a hug," she said. "And you know this guy was a big guy – he had tattoos all over his back and his arms – and when I gave him a hug he just . . . cried. He just cried. And he said, 'How could such a little woman bring me down to tears?' And I told him, 'You know, the Creator gave you tears to wash out your eyes and clean out your heart.'"

Now she and I both had moist eyes. Rose smiled at me as I swiped my tears away and said, "I'm really like that, too. And there's nothing wrong with tears . . . do you want another coffee?"

As we stood up at the coffee bar, Rose looked around the café. She said that she loves this place, but it doesn't bring in enough money for them to survive. They'd even gotten to a point recently when they were desperate, when payments on the Keewatin Station could no longer be met. That's when, said Rose, the spirits brought her a steady job teaching in the North each winter to supplement their income. "The spirits look after us when we can do our best," she nodded.

I asked her why she doesn't write a book on the plants and sell it out of the Keewatin, and at bookstores and through Métis organizations around the province. "I don't know," she said, looking genuinely perplexed. "I don't know if I'm *supposed* to. And the thing is, I could tell people a lot about plants, but it's not only the plant. The plant is good in itself, but it's the energy that's put in there – it's like me *and* the plant *and* the Creator. It's like mixing bannock. We can all use the same recipe, but each one will be different. People have different magic, we all have energy."

We sat down at our table again. "Like I've worked long and hard with medicines," said Rose, "and I only keep what the spirits feel that I should keep. I've had a lot of people coming in . . . like this Medicine Man came in and he said, 'I need lynx meat because I use it for cancer,' and I said, 'Hey, I've got some,' so I gave him some. And he came again and wanted more lynx meat, so I gave him some. And then he said, 'Okay here's how you use it for cancer,' and he gave me the instructions on how to use it, but I ended up telling him, 'Listen, that's *yours*, that's your medicine, not mine. If you use that to help people, then you use it, but until it's given to me by the spirits, I don't want to use it.'"

Rose has treated people with cancer and AIDS though, using her own medicines. "I've been working with a lot of people that have cancer. I've been giving them chaga, a fungus from the birch. Native people use it as prevention, but they use chaga in China and Russia, too. I had a vision that it's good for AIDS, so I've been also giving it to people who have AIDS."

I'd heard she has helped many people regain their health. I was curious if she would make medicine for anybody and everybody, or if she is selective.

"Well, some people come in and want things I don't agree with," she said slowly. She shook her head. "Like this one guy wanted love medicine – and I won't even *make* stuff like that, because it's manipulative. And sometimes people come in and I look at them and I feel really repulsed, I don't know what it is. So I don't make them medicine, I'll make an excuse." She shrugged, adding, "Or I just won't know! That's it, I just won't *know* what to make."

The café suddenly darkened. We both turned to look out the window; the sky had turned grey with ominous rainclouds. There was a current of potential in the air, like something could happen.

"You know," she offered, "one of the biggest drains on me is negative energy. It just hurts me so bad. It's so hard on me." Sometimes, said Rose, when people come in to the restaurant and she senses their negative energy, she will cleanse it from them. "They don't even know I'm doing it," she said. "I go over to them, and I may sit down beside them in a chair, and I end up holding the back of their chair like this," she said, with her right arm draped over the back of the empty chair beside her, "and asking how their day is going. But I'm drawing the energy away from them like this." Her right hand was face down, in a brushing movement. "You can feel that negative energy, you can *feel* it. Sometimes your spirit can see it.

"Like you can feel people without touching them," she said, rising from her chair and walking around behind me. "A lot of times the negative energy collects at the back," she said, brushing the air down from the top of my shoulders. "So you just sweep it," she said gently, with subtle movements of her hand, "just take it away." I felt a distinct coolness running down my back as her hand swept the air down. "If somebody's negative and they're angry, then all of a sudden everybody is. So you try to break that right away."

Rose walked back to her chair and sat down. She spoke about radio and TV being so negative these days that she doesn't turn them on. Instead, she said, she meditates and reads. "I read almost anything," she smiled, "but I especially like horror and supernatural stories, and I like to read them when I'm on my own." The room lit up in a sudden flash, and then a loud crack of thunder shook the café. We laughed at the timing.

"So horror stories don't scare you?" I was impressed, having been haunted myself for some 25 years by certain scenes from *The Changeling* and *The Shining*.

"Hardly anything scares me," she said, quietly. "I get attracted, and drawn to it. Like one time driving to Meadow Lake, I saw these two lights hovering above the trees over in the distance. And I drove really fast and I was going to go take a close look at it, I was going to stop the vehicle and see what it was. And the next thing you know I was in Meadow Lake. Just stopped on the road, and I was like, 'How did I get here?'" She shook her head in puzzlement. "I don't know what happened," she said almost ruefully, like she'd missed out on an important experience.

"The oddest things have always happened in my life," Rose continued, clearly wanting to talk about this. "Like if something odd doesn't happen this week or this month, I'll think, 'What did I do wrong?' I'll miss it," she grinned. The café door opened, and a woman with two children walked in. Rose paused, looking like she might need to get up, but Ric was quickly over greeting the new visitors and offering them some lunch.

"When I was a little kid," Rose said softly, "I used to see things that I didn't know other people didn't see. I saw my aunt in her coffin about six months before she died. And I remember she sat in the coffin and she looked at me and smiled – and I saw her through the blankets when I covered my head in my bed. She looked at me and smiled, then she went back into the coffin and it closed. My mom woke up and I told her what I'd seen. And my mom went around putting nails on the windows – she figured somebody had tried to come in, and *that's* what I'd seen. But I didn't know that she didn't see it. Like when you're a kid, you don't know that people have their own perceptions and see differently."

I was starting to realize that the term 'folk healer' didn't fully encompass Rose. Oh, I certainly believed she could help people with her plant medicine. But her gift was informed by something greater; her guidance came from the spirit world. She was able to access other dimensions. I was now thinking she would more aptly be described as a mystic, someone who is able to experience realities beyond normal human comprehension.

The newest arrivals to the restaurant were set up with cold drinks and homemade pie, so Ric came back over to our table and sat down.

"Me and my brother used to play ball with the Little People," Rose said, smiling with the memory. "This was in Meadow Lake. I really liked that place. We'd play ball, and every evening those kids would come. We were playing ball but we'd never talk – we'd laugh a lot and we'd communicate. It was later on I realized that we never *did* talk, we laughed a lot and we were happy. One evening I came in and my sister said, 'Who are those kids that you were playing with?' So I ran out to ask the kids where they were from. They were gone. And we lived in a … like it was flat, it was a meadow, so we should have seen them walking yet, but they were gone. And where they got the ball and bat from, God only knows. But my sister saw them too, and my brother was there and we actually played ball with them."

I had heard of fairies and elves, but I hadn't heard specifically of the Little People. "Are the Little People like leprechauns or something?" I asked.

"Yes," said Ric. "Every culture's got Little People. There's many stories of Little People in aboriginal culture. They make reference to them every now and then, because they also give great gifts."

Rose was still remembering her old playmates. "This one kid wore a tweed jacket, a tweed hat and tweed shorts. Wherever he was from, I don't really know. Because we didn't dress like that, only he did. And after my sister asked me where the kids were from, they never came back."

But, she said, she's had more encounters with the Little People since. "Like this one time, I lost my car keys for a whole month. I searched the entire house, the dressers, everything, I searched all over. And it was getting to be a problem not having a car to drive anywhere. And then finally after a month, I said out loud in the house, 'Okay, the game is over, you can *have* the car, that's it,'" she said, grinning. "You know, 'The car is yours, so now you didn't steal it, and you're not hiding it on me because it's *yours*.' Then I left. And when I came back home, the keys were on the bed. Right on the centre of the bed." She chuckled, saying she figured the Little People were calling her a poor loser.

Ric said this happened just a couple years ago. He added that being able to see the Little People, and knowing about the plants are special gifts. "It's different in the non-Native world where you just go to school to learn about things. In our culture, you have to be chosen."

I could see why Rose might be chosen; there was definitely something very special about her. I wanted to stay longer, but I saw the rain was now beating down on the highway in torrents. I said I had better get going back to our cabin. Rose suggested that since the cabin was only an hour away, we should see each other more often. If my husband was busy building, she offered, I could drive up and have coffee with her.

As I drove back that day I felt energized and alive, amazed by the wonders of the natural world. A whim had me parking the truck, and slogging through the wet ditchgrass over to a breathtaking patch of bluebells serenely braving the downpour. These sweet little flowers are also known as lungwort; they are a medicine for the lungs. I breathed deep.

* * *

Several weeks later, I found myself driving south past Green Lake on the way back to Saskatoon after a long day in Meadow Lake. I was tired and still had nearly four hours of driving ahead of me. But the Keewatin Station looked so charming, plus I wanted to keep in touch with Rose and Ric . . . I parked and went into the cafe, and was welcomed warmly. Rose invited me to help myself to coffee.

They were busy these days, they said, getting prepared for another annual First Nation International Gathering for Medicines and Healing, happening the following week at Sweetgrass First Nation. I asked how such a gathering works. Do people pay the healers for their services?

"If people can offer me something, then they do," said Rose. "But if they can't, I help them anyway. Hopefully it will create its own balance in time. In terms of helping people, if we give what we can, then hopefully the Creator will turn around and give us what we need to survive also."

Meanwhile, she was cutting me a piece of Saskatoon pie. She'd tried a new recipe, adding some vanilla cake batter to the pastry, and she said she wanted my opinion on it. She brought it over to the table, complete with melting ice cream on top, and sat down with me. Ric went to make a phone call.

I was loving the spongy purple pie, and Rose was pleased. Meanwhile, I'd had some time to think about our last visit, and I wondered about something. She had talked about negative energy, and I wanted to know more. Like did she see things as positive and negative, good and evil?

"There's good and bad in this world and it only depends on the individual," she explained. "I can use these hands to do good and to help people, I can also use these hands to hurt people. I can use my speech to speak good about people or to hurt them. So it's all a matter of choice in terms of how you use things." She lowered her voice and spoke carefully. "I have worked with kids and some adults that were involved in negative stuff – like satanic ritual – I helped them get out of it. But that takes a long time, and it can be dangerous. It's a choice between good and evil. Some people *are* evil, a lot of times it's because they've been hurt themselves, a lot of times it's in terms of power.

"Like Ouija boards, tarot cards, palm-reading – they can all be dangerous," said Rose gravely. "Never open a portal unless you know how to get out of it. You don't know *what* you're calling, you don't know *who* you're calling. Those things are not for me – if people want to use them they can, but they're not for me. And I know I can read cards, I know I can read teacups, I know I can do a lot of things, but I choose not to. There's a time and place for everything, and this is just not it."

I nodded. Now finished the dessert, I thanked her for the treat. She smiled, then stood up from the table and invited me to come with her to the museum. "We can talk better back there," she said. "There's no distractions." I brought along my tape recorder and coffee and we sat at the round table, amidst the artifacts and history. I noticed that Rose's tone was now more hushed and personal.

She admitted she's been tired lately, and she needs to muster more energy before going to the healing gathering. There was something else . . . something bothering her. She'd been concerned about certain people coming to her for spiritual medicine recently; she'd been feeling the responsibility for making sure the medicines go to the right people.

"I need time to think about it, you know. Because I'm afraid that if the spirits give me information and it's meant to help certain people that have not asked for it yet, that if it's given away too freely to anybody and everybody . . . well, if it's spiritual medicine and if you give it to the wrong person they'll know how to destroy it."

She said when the medicine ends up in the wrong hands, it hurts her. "I suffer by being sick or just from knowing that I did something wrong. Or feeling a storm, you know, feeling that I'm on the edge of a storm."

Her voice dropped to barely more than a whisper. "Like I have medicine I work with in terms of – and this was almost like a vision, too – in terms of working with people that are involved in satanic ritual."

"To cleanse them?" I asked, fascinated. "To exorcise them?"

Rose paused. "To fight with Satan," she stated. "Where he fights me instead of fighting those people, where it's me and him fighting for this person – and I'll just get knocked over, he'll physically fight me. But it's things like that I don't want to expose my family to, you know. Like there was this girl that was involved in satanic ritual and it took me a long time to get it out of her, but some of the people that were around me ended up really suffering, you know. Because they get too involved in terms of being easily fooled or maybe being afraid, and it makes them vulnerable.

"And like, I'm intrigued by this, I get drawn to it, but how much can I get involved without family people saying, 'Well what is that medicine you're using, what did you put in that?' and I have to say, '*I can't tell you,*' you know, and then it's like, 'Why, don't you trust me?' Then that's a spiritual battle that's going into play, sometimes it becomes really difficult for me."

I listened to her, rapt. My limited concept of satanism had come only from horror films and a few sensationalized stories in the media over the years. But, in fact, the Catholic church treats possession by demons as a very real threat; so much so, the church has an official Rite of Exorcism for priests to banish evil spirits from people.

"So I make the medicine that I have to, but then . . . I get dragged down physically, and emotionally and spiritually. It becomes really hard. And you can't be afraid, you have to be strong."

I studied Rose solemnly, beginning to visualize more of this preternatural world that she lived in. She was like a virtuous warrior in age-old battles between black and white, wrong and right, evil and good; forces that are always at work, not just in fables and mythology and

Hollywood movies. With her allies – the wild plants and the spirits that guide her – giving her insight and vision, I now saw Rose as an animist soldier involved in a timeless struggle for . . . well, I guess for humanity. For the greater good.

"I was working with a girl involved with satanic ritual," Rose continued, slowly, "and all the furniture was shaking, the bed was shaking, and the girl was screaming and being afraid of me, you know. And I said, 'What did you see me as, to be so frightened?'" (Here I got a chill of excitement as I realized that Rose was asking the girl what form she had seen Rose in. I remembered years ago reading two or three books written by Carlos Castaneda, regarding the teachings of an elderly Yaqui Indian named Don Juan, who lived in the Arizona desert. According to Castaneda, Don Juan was a sorcerer or shaman, capable of shifting into animal form. This wasn't the first I'd heard of the phenomenon; in Native American mythology, there are many tales of 'shape-shifting.')

Rose went on, intently. "Then I took her and held her and said, 'You're okay, you're safe here.' And I sat on the bed and said, 'Whoever you are, leave. I'm not afraid of you.' Then the bed was shaking and everything was shaking, all the staff were afraid, and finally this woman comes up and she says, 'Rose open the window, whatever it is needs to escape, it's running from you in this room and has no way to get out because we're standing at the door praying.' And then I opened the window, you know, and it was gone."

Rose's gaze was penetrating. Her dark eyes held a spark in them that came from somewhere else. Simmering ancient volcanoes . . . .

"So afterwards I told this girl, 'I'll pray with you for a week at 9 o'clock every night, wherever I am, I'll pray,' and no matter what that girl was doing, 9 o'clock would come along and she'd lay down and she'd say, 'Rose is praying with me, Rose is praying with me.' But every night at 9 o'clock the phone would ring or somebody would come and then I'd have to find the time to go to a place where I could pray and play the drum . . . I was totally drained, there'd always be something to take me off course. Or I'd say, 'Okay, I'll come there to be with you,' but then the vehicle would break down or run out of gas. Something would happen to take me off course."

The tape recorder snapped off, indicating the cassette was full. I didn't put a new one in. We heard the restaurant door open and Ric talking to some customers. I was surprised when Rose said suddenly, "Come to my house, okay? It's just a few minutes down the road. But we can talk better there. I'd like to show you my teepee." I told her I didn't want to take more of her time if she needed to get back to work, but she was already taking off her apron and leading me back through the restaurant.

We drove the two miles to her home and turned in a gravel driveway. Out front, there was a pole flying a Métis Nation flag, and beside that, a large white teepee with a dozen lodgepoles sticking out the top like a spiky Mohawk haircut. Behind that, enshrouded in luxuriant foliage and vines, was the long, wood-sided house. She showed me her beautiful flowers – gargantuan delphiniums and dense, flowering clematis clustered around the wooden deck. At the back of the house was a green lawn leading down to a river, with a red canoe waiting on the bank. It was as charming and attractive a place as the Keewatin Junction.

Rose invited me inside. We sat at her kitchen table with a big bowl of bannock dough rising between us, and looked out over the back lawn. It was late afternoon with slowly falling light; it was quiet, hot, and still. There was no sound except our soft voices, telling stories – one was about the black bear who regularly visited her backyard and whom she talked to – and sharing some intimacies about our personal lives. I felt honoured to be invited into Rose's inner sanctum. I felt flattered that she wanted to know me better, wanted my opinion on things, wanted to show me her world.

But I felt something else, too. Our eyes were locked the whole time on one another's; that's where the information was, the eyes as windows to the soul. And although the connection was friendly – even affectionate – there was a starkness in being so profoundly seen. It was the same, stripped feeling I had once when I couldn't break eye contact with a huge black wolf at the Saskatoon Forestry Farm.

And I don't know how to describe this, but I felt like I was outside of my body. I could hear what Rose and I were saying, but our conversation was secondary; distant. I don't know if it was the heat – it was such a humid, sweltering day – but in that space, it seemed like we had transcended our physical selves. Like it was our souls that were doing the visiting. To truly connect with this woman who communes with plants, who speaks to bears, who shapes energies and shifts her own form . . . was an intense experience. To be present in a place that allows for aliens, entities and Little People was surreal.

In fact, it was suddenly overwhelming. My pulse started to race, I began to sweat, I felt light-headed. Rose was still speaking calmly about the spirit world, and it was then I realized I had not been ready for this. I didn't prepare myself, I didn't ground myself; these were deeper waters than I'd ever swam in before.

I disengaged from our gaze, and looked out the back window to the simple green grass and the contented cat sitting on the deck. I took a deep breath. And another. Then I turned back to look at Rose's serene, smiling face and said, "Rose, I should be going now. I still have to drive back to Saskatoon tonight." She agreed, and said she'd come back with me to the Keewatin.

Once there, I went inside to get the rest of my papers and to say good-bye to Ric while Rose went into the kitchen. She soon came out with a bannock bun piled high with hot roast beef and melted cheese. It was on a Styrofoam plate, wrapped in cellophane. "For your drive home," she said, grinning. And indeed I was hungry; it had been a long trip. She also gave me a Ziploc bag full of bannock for my husband.

On my way home, once more exhilarated and inspired, I thought about the experience I'd just had at Rose's house. I recalled that Carlos Castaneda, during his apprenticeship with Don Juan, wrote about altered states of consciousness. These mind states were temporary, induced by any number of factors including prayer, psychoactive plants, and sensory deprivation. They were a powerful method used to see differently, to learn something that couldn't be experienced with the everyday consciousness.

And I supposed that's what had happened to me for a few moments, when Rose brought me into her spiritual space. There I caught a glimpse into an epic world of demons and angels, of plants and magic, of ritual and reverence, of energy and light. A macrocosm of metaphysics and miracles.

Rose, I believe, had opened what William Blake called "the doors of perception," and in a sublime act of revelation, she had invited me in.

Into the mystic.

WISDOM OF THE SAGES

"Governing sense, mind and intellect, intent on liberation, free from desire, fear and anger, the sage is forever free."

From the *Bhagavad Gita*

You can still hear the British influence in Jai Ram's accent; it smoothes the singsong lilt of his native Hindi tongue. His graciousness and openness and warmth are immediate. "Please come in, Jacquie, come in!" he urges, at the door of his White City bi-level home. I thank him for inviting me in. He says he hopes I had no trouble finding his house – I assure him his verbal directions were easy to follow – and then he apologizes for the jumble of shoes and toys in the entryway. His daughter and grandson are visiting from Toronto and his grandson has left items all over the house, he explains, clearly delighted.

While I carefully place my sandals out of the way in the corner, I notice Jai Ram is wearing a lovely, patient smile. I smile back at him deferentially. And now we are in it: that dance of social mirroring, where one generously polite individual inspires an elevated courtesy in others, too. I make a brief mental 'Post-It' to practice more cordiality in my own everyday interactions.

Briefly, I breathe in the complex medley of Indian incense and spices in the house, take a quick glance at the rich red and gold textures on the walls and floors. I must admit, I'm an India groupie. I love the exalted flavours and exotic dishes of Indian cuisine; it resonates perfectly with my palate. I'm enamoured with the colourful woven fabrics and sequined scarves; Indian textiles thrill my inner princess. I'm entranced by the twisting voice of the sitar, the metallic thrum of the tabla in India's most ancient of harmonies. And in my university Religious Studies class some 15 years ago, I was particularly intrigued by the spirituality of India – Hinduism – considered to be the oldest religion still being practiced today, with its beginnings pegged sometime around 1500 BCE. The *Bhagavad Gita*, Hinduism's sacred text, is full of poetry and allegory which manages to remain timelessly relevant.

Hinduism incorporates many gods and goddesses. Interestingly, these deities are usually portrayed in paintings and sculptures with their hands prominently shown, palms up. Open palms, it is thought, accept All; open hands receive the Universe. As well, the palms are portals to knowledge – knowledge of the world, tactile and sensual, and knowledge of the self.

"The hand, literally, is the instrument of your brain," Jai Ram had told me over the phone. "Whatever you think, whatever you do, is registered in your palm."

In the ancient Indian or Vedic tradition, hand analysis is called "Hasta Samudrika Shastra." Translated, this means "the precepts of the signs, symbols, and seals of the hand, which are as large as an ocean." This tradition is thousands of years old; the sacred information is generally passed on from mentors to apprentices. According to Hasta Samudrika Shastra, our hands are like mirrors, even more expressive than our faces. Within the lines and markings of our hands and fingers is the story of our life – our background, personality style, health, careers, relationships, and spirituality.

"Of all the sciences, this is as close as you will ever come to knowing yourself," Jai Ram had assured me. Hand analysis can help identify one's talents and strengths, as well as potential pitfalls and weaknesses. The purpose is to help people gain personal insight and live more gratifying lives. Or, as it is written in the *Bhagavad Gita*:

> *Sever the ignorant doubt in your heart with the sword of self-knowledge.*
> *Observe your discipline.*
> *Arise.*

Jai Ram now politely ushers me down the carpeted stairs to the lower level, and into his office. As I step in, I'm somewhat taken aback. The large room looks like a university library after a particularly animated study session. There are shelves upon shelves of tomes and texts and sets of hardcover reference books, while piles of newspaper articles and letters cover every chair or desk surface, and boxes of books and papers crowd the floor. It is not dirty or slovenly, but it is most certainly kinetic. Some would even say 'chaotic,' but I soon discover that Jai Ram knows exactly where every book and article is buried. "Please, Jacquie, take a seat there," he smiles and gestures to one of two chairs in front of a heavily burdened wooden desk.

Jai Ram sits in the other chair a couple of feet away, and faces me. He asks me to hold my hands up for him to see, then he positions the head of a desk lamp to point directly at my palms, and looks into them. With a pencil held lightly in his right hand he points, without touching, to the markings and characteristics in each of my hands. "The left hand is the karmic hand," he explains. "Unless you're left-handed, then it's reversed."

In Hinduism, karma literally means action, and refers to the universal principle of cause and effect, or action and reaction, which applies to all life. It can be physical action or mental action (thought). But the jist of it is, what you sow you will reap. With the right intent and thinking and deeds, one will enjoy good circumstances in life. I often refer to karma myself: a series of bad-luck incidents is simple 'karma cleansing'; and "What goes around, comes around" is one of my standard aphorisms. The *Bhagavad Gita* illustrates karma more eloquently:

> *In battle, in the forest, at the precipice in the mountains;*
> *On the dark great sea, in the midst of javelins and arrows;*
> *In sleep, in confusion, in the depths of shame;*
> *The good deeds a man has done before defend him.*

"The lines on your hand are the map of your life," says Jai Ram. "Of your previous lives, your previous activities, and what you brought into this life. And that's why, for example on your own hands, the lines are not the same. So your karmic hand will show what you could have done, your potential – those lines are preordained. The lines manifest when you are born, they come with you. But they do change to some extent; they are modified, they grow, they disappear. And your right hand will show what you *are* doing with your life now. As you grow in life and you are involved in activities, it will show what you're doing right and what you're not doing right."

It's important to note that karma is not fate. Because humans are able to act with free will, it is thought, they create their own destinies. As well, Hindus believe in reincarnation and the possibility of multiple lives; the principle of karma incorporates our actions from this life, as well as any previous lives, to determine our fortunes today and tomorrow. As far as principles go, karma represents the pinnacle of personal responsibility and personal freedom – do what you will, but know there will always be consequences.

"Sometimes the hands will show great variations, left to right," Jai Ram explains. "If the right hand has good lines, is a good positive hand, it shows that you have beaten the background – the family circumstances, the area you were born if it was underprivileged – and you have improved immensely. And that itself is an indicator of the next life, also of moving to a higher conscious level. If the lines on your right hand are poor," he says in contrast, "that means you are not taking advantage of all the faculties you were given. You've wasted all that opportunity."

Although there are karmic consequences for squandering one's potential, there is no threat of eternal damnation. Most Hindus believe that all souls eventually do reach the highest levels of consciousness – it's just that for some, it may take millions of rebirths to get there.

Now comparing my karmic hand to my 'real' hand, Jai Ram begins the reading. "You take nothing for granted," he says emphatically, "because nothing was given to you on a platter. You had to work for everything. You are very independent," he states, "very independent, and this was formed out of protection for yourself. Please confirm," he says, now raising his eyes to meet mine. I agree that this is accurate; he looks down into my palms and continues.

"There was no support when you were young, so you had to become self-sufficient. You are practical and self-guided." I nod.

"In fact, around the age of 30, you found your very own path in life. This is when you became fully independent." *Yes I suppose that's true*, I think to myself. At 30, I ended a long relationship, bought my own little house, and scrapped the 9-to-5 job model to cultivate a simple lifestyle which could be maintained on freelance work alone. That's when I consciously began to customize my own life.

He turns my palms to look at a certain angle, then chuckles warmly. "You didn't have it easy financially when you were young either, but it's much better now. You weren't born into fortunate circumstances," Jai Ram says, shaking his head, "but you overcame this with your own mental fortitude, and so you will want for nothing." He smiles at me, then clarifies his statement. "You won't be rich, but you'll want for nothing." I understand this completely and I agree. For instance, I do still wear second-hand clothes but now it's because I choose to.

Jai Ram looks at the inside of my wrist and pronounces: "You had a deep fear of water when you were younger, and you almost perished in it once."

Wow! Just yesterday, I was recounting to a friend my childhood terror of water. The paintings I did in nursery school and kindergarten would often be an entire sheet of black or dark blue, with a little dot of pink in the middle. The caption, blithely penned in large and perfect teacher's lettering, would read, "This is someone drowning," or "This is a girl drowning." Then, one summer day when I was about eight, my cousin and I rowed an inflatable raft out to the middle of Round Lake, and with no supervision or lifejackets, started jumping off together into the deep water. Neither of us noticed the wind picking up until, in an instant, a forceful gust sent the empty raft skimming and somersaulting across the lake. *Gone.* An instinctive and desperate dog-paddle, fuelled by a flood of adrenaline, propelled me eventually (I'm sure it took at least a half-hour) to the shallows. I've thought about it many times since. That day could easily have turned out very differently.

Now I look at this learned man who elicits such information from my hands. At 74, he is slight – not quite my height (nor my weight, I bet!) – but his body is strong. Behind his glasses, his large brown eyes are ravaged by a grey cloudiness. I suspect that his eyesight is rather diminished . . . but not his vision. Most notable about Jai Ram is his energy, enthusiasm, and passion. Especially about palmistry.

"Palmistry requires a very deep study of the subject," he asserts. "Professional palmists take thousands of palm prints to hone their abilities." He stands up to rifle through a precarious mountain of papers nearby on the sofa and immediately locates several palm prints he was recently sent by clients. On the photocopies, he points out how subtle changes can be documented over time. "This is not black magic." He enunciates each word forcefully. "It is a science."

One that he's been learning for some 60 years. He grew up in a small farming community in the Himalayas in India. The village priest or 'pundit' saw in the young Jai Ram a gift, and told him he must study palmistry. "The pundits are temple priests, but they are very well-versed in palmistry and astrology," explains Jai Ram. "For example, as you walked in here, they would tell you a great deal about yourself merely by the way you stepped and the way your hands moved. And by face readings." So the village pundit began to mentor the young Jai Ram. "This went on for a while and then, when I was 12 or 13, I was sent to England to go to school. And there I continued to learn. I began to seek books, but I also sought the help of some palmists who were living in London."

In his professional life, he earned a PhD in Business Management from the University of Sussex. Until now, I hadn't realized he had a doctorate. After university he was enlisted in the British Air Force; Dr. Ram tells me only that "those were very difficult years." Later, he moved to Regina where he received a B.Ed from the University of Regina. Since 1976, he taught Business Law and many other subjects at the Saskatchewan Institute of Applied Science and Technology, from which he's only recently retired. Although he has never advertised, he has analyzed palms for people from all around the world. "Every three or four years I go to India, go to the temples and seek some help from the pundits," he tells me.

"So you're still learning palmistry?" Considering his age, I'm a little surprised.

"All the time, all the time, all the time," declares Dr. Ram enthusiastically. "There was a time when I was training and I was learning and I would be sitting in the bus or on the train, and always looking at people's hands, because this is part of being inquisitive. But my learning, it will never stop. Never stop. In fact, Indian palmistry is so deep, even your lifetime is not enough to learn everything."

As he speaks, I recall the essence of a Hindu proverb: *"A man in this world without learning is as a beast of the field."*

Dr. Ram is leaning over the crowded desktop, and now pulls out a thin book from somewhere in the middle. "For instance, recently I was in India and this is a little book I picked up on analyzing specifically the thumb. The thumb bones, for example, can show how old you are because the thumb is like a tree stump with its ring for each year. But you know," he says with a wry smile, "you can just ask a person's age so who has time?"

"This," he says, holding up an index finger for significance, "is the most essential part." I respond to his professorial cue by picking up my pen and pad to write down whatever he is about to divulge. "It's all very good intellectually exercising our minds, it's good because that is advancement of knowledge," he says. "But if that knowledge, Jacquie, cannot be transferred into usefulness, then you're wasting your time. So palmistry *guides* people, *shows* people how to lead productive and better lives.

"Let me give you examples. If I see in the hand that there is illness, it will show at what phase in life, at what time during the lifespan this is likely to manifest. So you guide people, you say, 'Look, at that particular age you will have problems, now this is what you need to do to prevent that.' Supposing you see someone who is going through emotional upheavals, the hand will show that. So we guide them. 'Look, these areas are affecting you, you need to do this, this and this.' Or supposing someone is going through very difficult financial problems, the hand will show that. Whether the individual is just wasting their money or not working properly or not holding a job, we guide the individual. Supposing there's married life, someone is going through difficulty, we would be able to guide the person and say, 'Look, your problem lies here and this is what you need to do.'"

Like any accomplished orator, Dr. Ram uses silence as much as speech to hold his listener's attention. "So it's a practical application of palmistry for daily living," he states vigorously. "It's not just knowledge for the sake of knowledge, which is also very good – nothing wrong with that – but that must be translated into usefulness."

I am in wholehearted agreement. Satisfied that his present student has assimilated the tutorial part, Dr. Ram says he can now interpret the data in my palms and perhaps suggest means of achieving more equilibrium in my life. Noting the propensity in my family for heart disease and high blood pressure, he suggests that I quit eating red meat and even become vegetarian. He procures from one of the floor-to-ceiling bookshelves a thick text on Indian vegetarian cooking – something about Lord Krishna's favourite recipes – and thumbing through the pages, shows me the multitude of sumptuous and healthy recipes therein. We flip past cauliflower and green pea samosas, curried potatoes with eggplant, baked bananas stuffed with tamarind coconut . . . now famished, I make a silent plan that when I leave here my immediate destination will be an Indian restaurant in Regina.

Then sitting back down to face me, Dr. Ram is vehement in his encouragement that I go back to university. He states I have strong mental capabilities and a good aptitude for facts, communication and learning; clearly, he is a man who is ardent about higher learning.

He also informs me I will travel a lot in my life, even as an old woman, and will live well into my 80s. Good enough for me.

Dr. Ram then addresses the issue of my oversensitivity. How I tend to take things too personally which, he says, causes me undue strife. To balance this out, he recommends I make a daily practice of yoga. He says the stretching calms the central nervous system, while the meditative aspect helps foster a non-attachment and a non-emotionality towards the impermanent moments of life. I already know this to be true; once a week I do a two-hour yoga and meditation class, after which I feel at my ultimate best, both physically and mentally. A daily practice of yoga would change my life, undoubtedly. As the *Bhagavad Gita* puts forth, under "The Way of Love":

> *Better indeed is knowledge than mechanical practice.*
> *Better than knowledge is meditation.*
> *But better still is surrender of attachment to results,*
> *because there follows immediate peace.*

Dr. Ram invites me to ask specific questions. For once, I have none. It has all been crystal clear to me and makes perfect sense. There were no surprises. None except for the simple fact that this complete stranger could know me so fundamentally by looking into my palms for 30 minutes. He tells me this reading is now complete and if I want, I can come back in a year or more to monitor the changes.

We leave his office and walk down the hall to the staircase. En route, Dr. Ram invites me to see his in-home temple on this lower level. It is a recessed ledge built into the wall, 18 inches deep at chest level, with sacred and ritual effects placed on it. Lord Krishna is represented there, as is the supreme goddess Radharani. There is a conch shell, which Hindus believe resonates with "the primordial sound of creation." And there are the items of the daily offering to the Hindu deities: flowers, a glass of water, incense, clarified butter and a peacock feather. In front of this altar, Dr. Ram does his yoga every morning at 5 a.m., seven days a week. And it is there that he meditates. It is a simple, yet profound space. And I am instantly inspired: I could easily arrange an area of serenity like this in my own house, too.

Dr. Ram sent me home that day with a copy of the award-winning cookbook *Lord Krishna's Cuisine: The Art of Indian Vegetarian Cooking,* an 800-page veritable encyclopedia to help me incorporate non-meat dishes into my diet. Meanwhile, since my return home I have converted our spare bedroom into a yoga and meditation studio. And thanks to Dr. Ram's encouragement, I enrolled in university for the first time in 15 years.

It's all about working within your own limitations, I understand, but the goal is to explore what the outer edges of those might be. As age-old wisdom puts it:

There is nothing noble in being superior to some other man.
The true nobility is in being superior to your previous self.

And so there is another cultural treasure to add to my list of Indian enchantments: the Vedic art of hand analysis to help navigate one's life. Guidance at your fingertips, and answers in the palm of your hand.

THE CHRYSALIS

It was an 'alar' experience. All about wings. To begin with, it was the summer of the cabbage worm in Saskatchewan – made manifest through millions of white and yellow butterflies. *Everywhere*. The wings of this particular species of butterfly are delicate, fluttery and soft. In complete contradiction, however, the creature's movement is choppy and erratic. These ubiquitous insects seemed to dart drunkenly out in front of anything moving; the front half of our truck was covered in a shiny butterfly shellac all summer.

And on that Thursday afternoon, as I drove the two kilometres from Milestone to Elizabeth Johnston's farmhouse, I also noticed an abundance of birds around; there were crows and swallows and hawks and magpies. Then when I pulled into Elizabeth's yard, a mourning dove was the greeter – I'd never seen them in the wild before. The yard was an oasis, with painted "Welcome" signs and birdhouses amidst a butterfly garden of colourful flowers and shrubs. A canopy of mature trees created coolness and shade, and helped to camouflage an attractive forest-green bungalow.

I was apprehensive as I got out of the truck. I had talked to Elizabeth twice on the phone, and I'd had a difficult time understanding what she was saying. She had a garbled way of speaking, and I thought I detected exasperation when I kept asking her to repeat herself. She had informed me in our conversation that she did emotional healing. Indeed, I'd heard about her, and her famous mother, from several sources. I asked her how long a session would be. She answered, "As long as it takes." (This, too, gave me concern; I wasn't sure if I'd ever see my home again.)

Elizabeth opened the door for me, then immediately turned and lurched back into the house, on stiff legs spread several feet apart. She was mumbling something about swallows and butterflies, but I didn't catch it. I'll be honest: I was somewhat alarmed by her speech and her gait. She roughly grabbed at furniture and walls as she stumbled past a pretty little half-bathroom and into a bright living room.

I kicked my sandals off by the door, and caught up to her. The living room had been turned into a waiting room, with five or six chairs positioned around the perimeter, and her desk and reference library in the corner. It was a welcoming space with picture windows, French doors and plush carpets. There was lots of eye candy about – dried flowers, scented candles, cherub figurines. Elizabeth staggered through this room to a hall, then stopped and clumsily motioned me into the first bedroom off to the right. I stepped past her and sat down gingerly on the tall, springy hospital bed, which had been covered with a white, fitted plastic sheet. She indicated that I should lie down.

Elizabeth shakily positioned herself on a rolling stool at the foot of the bed. She touched my bare feet with her cool hands and drawled, "You have a good energy." I smiled at her, felt myself relax a little. Now observing her fully for the first time, I was struck by her physical appearance: Elizabeth was a true beauty. In her mid 50s, she was a Jacqueline Onassis look-alike with the same wide-set eyes, high cheekbones, strong jaw, and well-coiffed shoulder-length hair. She was trim and fit, in a snug t-shirt and stylish slacks that showed her fantastic figure. Her refined looks did not correlate to her jerky body movements and coarse communication.

As she gruffly worked her knuckles into some painful points of my feet, I noticed the wall to my left showcased a large poster. It was an essay focusing on the thesis statement that 'emotional layering' actually affects and modifies the physiology of the body. I was already familiar with the work of Dr. Candace Pert, an American neuroscientist. Earlier in the summer, I'd seen her interviewed in the film, *What the Bleep Do We Know!?* Over the past two decades, Dr. Pert has been decoding the body's information molecules – such as neuro-peptides and their receptors – which regulate every facet of human physiology. Her model of how these biochemicals distribute information to every cell in the body has shown that emotions literally transform our anatomy and affect our health. In fact, this peptide network reaches into all the organs, glands, spinal cord, and tissues of the body which, according to Dr. Pert, means "that emotional memory is stored throughout the body. And you can access emotional memory anywhere in the network."

That poster reminded me of a study I'd recently heard of which explored the phenomenon of organ transplant recipients suddenly taking on the characteristics of their deceased (and anonymous) donors. Flinching while Elizabeth probed my feet, I recalled that in many cases food cravings, personality traits, hobbies, and even sexual preference changed after transplant surgery. Especially poignant was the story of a little girl who received the heart of another little girl who had been murdered. The recipient started having such traumatic nightmares about being violently killed, she was taken to a psychologist. Through her vivid description of a man, what he was wearing, the place and the time, and the exact weapon used, the actual murderer was found and convicted. It was a dramatic example of cellular memory.

I turned back to Elizabeth and said, "Do you believe what's on that poster? That our thoughts and emotions actually affect our physical body?"

"Of course they do," said Elizabeth. "For instance," she said, squeezing my baby toes, "I can see by these toes that when you were born, you looked up at the faces around you in the room for support – and there was none." She shrugged a little sadly as she said it.

I was taken aback with her assertion. This was a heavy statement to start with, and a dealbreaker if she was wrong. But I am well aware of my birth history, and she wasn't wrong. I settled in and began to trust her.

Then Elizabeth informed me my stomach 'pulls up' when I'm nervous. I raised my eyebrows in inquiry, so she stood up and precariously moved over to my side. She showed me how to make a fist in my diaphragm, then work it downward and end in an upward 'j' swoop. To create a vacuum, she said; to make space so my stomach could shift back down. I probably winced at the pressure of her fist in my gut, because it prompted her to explain: "A healer," she said, peering down into my face, "is one who points you in a direction, not one who makes the pain go away."

Her slurred speech and sleepy eye movements were reminiscent of one hampered by the effects of alcohol. But her sharp intellect made clear that this was not the case. "Because what is pain, anyway?" she continued, philosophically. "It's a symptom of something that needs to be looked at. How you react to things tells you about the issues you have, if you know how to listen."

She said she had a client one day who couldn't lift her arm. In talking to her, Elizabeth discovered that this woman had lost eight friends in the past two months. "I didn't even touch her," Elizabeth said, shaking her head. "I just had her face her feelings about losing so many people in her life . . . and her arm was healed."

Then she told me my green eyes mean I have courage. She said she also saw a green mist around me which, she said, indicated the angel Gabriel is with me. "You have lots of healing around you, lots of green. Whether that's the way it is, or the way *you* are, I don't know." Stooped forward and leaning on the bed for support, she felt her way back to the stool. She shakily sat down, took my feet in her hands, then looked at me.

"I got a message before you came," she announced, abruptly. "You have parasites. Do you travel?"

Stammering a bit, I answered, "Uh yeah, I guess – I was in Turkey last year." Thinking back, I realized I was in Mexico the year before, Bali not long before that . . . it was certainly possible I might have picked up something. Elizabeth instructed me to go to a specific health food store in my Saskatoon neighbourhood, and the parasite cleanse would be right there when I walked in the door. Her farm in southern Saskatchewan was hours away from this particular store, but having shopped there a couple days ago, I knew she was correct about the display by the door.

She now told me to take my silver toe-ring off and to keep it off. "It's strangling your centre of *doing*," she explained. And then added, "It's all about energy. Everything in life is energy." As she rigorously worked her fingers into my feet, I lay back to try and relax.

At one point I heard Elizabeth mutter something about having "lost the ceremony." I brought my elbows up on the bed to rest on and asked her what she meant. She said that in a previous time, she had sat in a cave and people came to her to rid themselves of negative energy, which she would extinguish with a certain ceremony. But, she said, she cannot remember it now.

"So, without that ceremony, what happens with the negative energy?" I asked her.

"Well, *look* at me!" she snorted.

"You mean, negative energy is making you . . .," I started. "Do you know what the problem is, exactly?" I asked, softly.

"Ataxia," she answered, bluntly.

"What is ataxia?" I cocked my head.

"It affects balance and speech," she slurred.

"Oh. When did you get it?"

"Five years ago. When I was 50."

"Is it getting worse as time goes on?"

"No, it's getting better. I'm already better than I was."

"So Elizabeth, can you overcome this ataxia?"

"I'll have relief from it in two years," her head bobbed, firmly. "I've been told that. I don't worry about it at all."

She directed me to stand up, so I swung my legs over the side of the bed and stood up on the laminate floor. "Unlock your knees," she said, leaning forward from her stool to wave at them. She told me to notice where my weight was resting on my feet. I thought it was evenly balanced between heel, instep and toes. She shook her head roughly in disagreement, then instructed me not to rest on my heels, but to bring the balance forward and stand on my toes. "Ready for life," she stated emphatically. And she told me my left shoulder was rounding forward, protecting my heart. "Bring it back, square off your shoulders."

Elizabeth repeated it twice before I understood she was now telling me to lie on my back on the bed. She said my pelvis was slightly skewed, making my perception of the world a little distorted. Well, I couldn't argue with that! She had me bend my knees, with my feet planted on the bed. Then she instructed me to pull my knees apart from each other, engaging the pelvis, while she pushed them together with her hands. I wasn't sure how much force to use, but despite her lack of coordination, she was surprisingly strong at applying direct pressure.

After a minute of this, we both took a breather. I asked her about her 88-year-old mother, Betty, whom I knew of. Betty wasn't at the farm these days, Elizabeth said; she was in B.C. Betty is another well-known energy worker who has been healing people for several decades now. Her focus is more physical than emotional, so mother and daughter worked together for years doing a holistic spectrum of healing.

"Mom, she's from the old school," Elizabeth explained. "Back when I was seven, she was already doing it, working out of the house. She was in court every week, they were always threatening to jail her because she didn't have a medical license to help people. This is why we never have files on clients – because the police took her files – and Mom said they have no business knowing personal things about these people." Elizabeth worked with her mother for 12 years and has worked the last five years on her own.

"So you started working on your own around the time you developed ataxia?" I said, starting to make a connection. Elizabeth nodded brusquely – she'd long ago made *that* connection – then made her way shakily to the foot of the bed and grasped the railing.

"I think the gift in this is that I slowed down and studied," she said. "In the old days I would see up to 50 people a day."

I shook my head in disbelief. "And you were healing them emotionally?"

"Yes. You do everything to make people more aware of who they are. Sometimes you don't need to do much, just help them acknowledge the emotion. To just look at it. And then *let it go*," she said, emphasizing each word with a nod of her head. "But however people are wounded, they must be helped. These days, I'll see someone for three or four hours if that's what it takes."

"You were helping 50 people a day?" I was incredulous.

"If it didn't work, people wouldn't come back," she answered frankly. "I've seen lots of deaths, too. Death being failure. But I've learned I cannot change it."

Some souls, said Elizabeth, aren't meant to be here a long time and there is nothing you can do about it, and it is perfectly natural and okay for these people to die prematurely. "One time, a baby was brought to me," she said, bending over the footrail to hold an imaginary baby's form on the bed. She demonstrated as she spoke: "And I was working on him, but the links weren't connecting, there was something wrong. And I could *see* that his soul was apart from his body." She raised her eyes to meet mine. "I looked over there," she said, waving at the chairs along the side wall, "and I saw his ancestors sitting, watching. So I asked them to put the baby's soul back in his body." She shook her head. "They said nothing." She looked to me again. "Soon after, the baby died," said Elizabeth, sighing deeply. "But on Christmas Eve that year, the baby came to me to explain the missing links, the things I couldn't make sense of at the time. And he told me he had never intended to live here for long, he'd only wanted to bring his family together. I was so elated, I called his mother right away and I said, 'It's okay, he wasn't meant to live any longer. He came to bring your family together' – and his death really *had* made them all closer. And I said to her," she added, releasing a hand from the footrail and wagging her index finger for emphasis: "'Do not miss this opportunity.'"

I digested the story for a moment.

"Elizabeth, why do you think the ataxia came on?"

"I don't feel worthy," she said, shrugging. She was certainly unafraid of emotional issues. "I knew I had the gift to heal, but I fought it. I have to learn to accept my gifts – I blocked them, at a deeper level. Now the healer needs to be healed. So when I work on you, I'm actually healing myself. I feel strong from working on people, I get a different energy."

I nodded slowly. Maybe after being under the shadow of her famous mother for all those years, Elizabeth was now recreating herself on her own terms. Like the cabbage worm butterfly, lovely Elizabeth was, today, physically erratic and ungainly. According to her, though, it was merely part of the process; the chrysalis was developing.

"I believe the reason I can't talk clearly right now is because I need to listen," she said, thoughtfully. "I always listen to what's around. Right now, it's hummingbirds. And swallows. And hawks are around me. I listen to the birds. They are the messengers between heaven and earth."

"The messengers between heaven and earth," I repeated. "That's really beautiful." I got up from the bed then, to follow Elizabeth out of the treatment room and down the hall. Was I imagining it or was she walking steadier now?

Back in the reception space, I noticed the abundance of angels – on shelves, in paintings, on her desk. And I was touched by the irony of Elizabeth's love for all the graceful, winged ones. Here she was, presently earthbound in the most clumsy and awkward way, her body threatening to come crashing down to the ground at any moment. However, Elizabeth believed this was simply a stage in her metamorphosis; in two years, her transformation would be complete and she would emerge in her glory.

In contrast to this year of the cabbage worm, I'm betting *that* will be the summer of something really special like the gossamer-winged Frosted Elfin butterfly. Or it might be the season of the dramatic Tiger Swallowtail; perhaps the cycle for the sparkly blue Spring Azure.

It may even be the time to herald in a brand new species for the Lepidoptera recordbooks. I can just imagine it: the Blue-Moon Elizabethan Angelwing. Its description will read: *"Sometimes called the First Lady of butterflies, this is a rare and exotic specimen found only in southern Saskatchewan; admired for its exquisite beauty and for its effortless grace of flight."*

But one thing I'm sure of: Elizabeth is getting her wings.

JOSEPH AND HIS
COAT OF MANY COLOURS

"Give a little more to the Moores next door, to restore their faith in this world once more."

From "Peace, Love and Harmony," the J. T. Styles band

I step into the Beverage Room of the one and only hotel in the village of Love, Saskatchewan. (You know you've gone rural when the bar is called a 'beverage room.') Once my eyes adjust to the dim light, I glance around to see several lit-up beer signs on wood-paneled walls, and a couple of ageing TVs hanging precariously in two of the room's corners. An array of cigarette burns like random buckshot scars the dark, patterned carpet, on top of which are a dozen or so brown laminate tables. A lone man sits at one, drinking a beer. In his early 50s, he's got a wild tangle of a beard underneath a well-worn cowboy hat. His leather vest and faded jeans look like they've put on a lot of miles with him.

As I slowly approach the bar, I stop beside his table and say, "I'm supposed to meet a friend named Joseph here. Have you seen him?"

He sizes me up with a glance and says, "'You Jacquie?" I laugh in surprise. (Another sign you've gone rural is when the only patron of the bar knows you're coming to town!) He introduces himself as Gunsmoke, and tells me Joseph is out at the cabin. Apparently Joseph's truck won't start, so he's asked Gunsmoke to provide me with directions there. "But I can only make you this map if you have a beer," deadpans Gunsmoke.

I happily order what he's having and take a seat across from him. The amiable bartender brings over two Coors Lights, along with a notepad and pen. I watch while Gunsmoke draws a comprehensive chart of the roads and landmarks (flavoured with colourful local history) that will guide me to the cabin.

I've driven three hours from Saskatoon today to spend some time with Joseph Hnatiw. I had met him at his family's Bruno farm one day last summer when I was there interviewing his mother, Pauline. Joseph had been dressed casually in cut-off jeans, a light blue t-shirt and flip-flop sandals – but he cut a striking figure. He was about 40, and his skin was so darkly tanned that it made his teeth and clear blue eyes gleam, while his shoulder-length hair was sun-bleached to a shiny gold. His voice was deep but notably gentle and softened – as if he were speaking to timid children and didn't want to scare them.

Joseph had been out at his parents' farm that day to drop off an old truck, and then he was planning to hitchhike back to Saskatoon. His mother had been so gracious to me, I was pleased to be able to offer him a ride. At the invitation, he'd beamed and kindly murmured, "Blessings to you."

The drive had been memorable, and was backdropped by a distinct musical score: as soon as we turned onto the highway, Joseph had asked if he could play me a CD. I liked the first song immediately; it had the vocal creaminess of Pink Floyd, layered over the country-rock grit of the Stones in their '70s prime. As it turned out, this was an original disc of the J.T. Styles band – and Joseph was J. T. Styles. With his David Gilmour-esque singing voice in the background, Joseph had serenely told me stories for the one-hour drive – but not in a domineering fashion. Rather, his words were an earnest offering; he spoke in the way of someone who reveled in the miracle of life, and was grateful for each moment in it. Someone who believed that every person deserves unconditional love, and who was constantly looking for ways that he could help others. And someone who referred sincerely – affectionately – to Jesus as his brother, and to God as his father. In normal conversation, and in everyday anecdotes, Joseph spoke of them as his highly respected family members. I'd never met someone so enthusiastic about God and Jesus unless . . . . "Joseph," I had ventured politely, "are you 'born again?'" To which this laid-back rock-and-roller had laughed and quipped: "No girl, I was *always* born!"

Joseph grew up on the farm in a large family, where he learned about hard work, sharing with others, caring for animals, gardening, and honouring God. "The family life we had was heavenly," his deep voice had purred. "We worked hard, and we ate off the farm. We had lots of animals – we hatched chicks and ducklings, we had calves and horses and dogs and cats. We kids looked after all the animals, and had a chance to see both life and death. We had foster children that lived with us too, so we learned – and this is important – that when you're with somebody and you grab a piece of bread, you need to first look around and ask, 'Anyone else want a piece of bread?' We grew up where if there was a chocolate bar, we all shared it. No one in our house was treated differently because of colour, no one was treated differently because of age – we were all equal on our farm. And that was a beautiful thing," he'd added, grinning at me.

I find the scenery from Bruno to Saskatoon is especially beautiful, and that day had been no exception. Off to the left, a strong and verdant field rippling in the breeze had drawn both of our gazes. Joseph looked blissful as he watched the natural world moving by. Then he'd shared more of his history.

At the age of 20, he nearly died in a serious car accident. The next seven years he spent in recovery, much of the time bedridden and disabled. With persistence and resourcefulness, he eventually regained his mobility and his strength. "It was a combination of a lot of different practitioners working on me, a lot of prayer, and a lot of beautiful people who came to my side and helped me out," he recounted with obvious gratitude.

I had been impressed by Joseph's altruism when he told me how he worked long hours cooking at Camp Easter Seals after his accident, while his back pain was debilitating. "Seeing those kids at camp made me realize what it was like to be *really* disabled," he said. "They didn't have any hope of recuperating or getting better." It helped him push on to heal himself. That experience – of being so physically damaged, and the process of rebuilding his health – gave him insights and techniques which he'd later used to perform healing body work on others. "Although that's a sideline," he'd added, looking over at me. "Not many people know I do body work."

When a gopher had suddenly scurried out of the ditch and across our lane, Joseph urged, "Run little guy, run!" With his short tail twitching wildly, the critter made the dash on stubby legs and we both laughed as he disappeared into the ditch on the other side.

Continuing to chat, Joseph had told me he just relocated to Tisdale a few years ago. Besides working as a carpenter, he was busy revitalizing the old Salvation Army building. "I had gotten a speeding ticket, and I wanted to work it off doing community service, so I chose the Salvation Army," he explained. "I was supposed to work 27 hours, but I put in about 150!" He laughed. He said he had taken out a wall in the old building, built a stage and put in a P.A. system. Now there was a space for community theatre and music. He'd also brought in a pool table, all sorts of instruments, and a projection TV.

The Salvation Army housed a drop-in centre for teens; to give them something creative to do, Joseph said, to give them an alternative to getting involved with gangs. So he and his bandmates started hosting regular music sessions with these local kids. With his guitarist, Jay Rock, he'd started up a Narcotics Anonymous group. "Basically we solved the problem of crystal meth use in Tisdale," said Joseph. "That drug was getting hold of lots of kids in town and I just wanted to help." He had glanced briefly to the right to see a red-winged blackbird sitting on a nearby fencepost. "I can talk to kids, be honest with them . . .," he said then, turning back to me. "And I've been down that road myself," he'd admitted.

He was teaching young people carpentry skills, and hiring them to assist him on jobs. With the renewed interest in the Salvation Army centre, there were more donations coming in, so Joseph said he spent a lot of time sorting through all the extras, then delivering boxloads of useful items out to surrounding Hutterite colonies and First Nation communities. In essence, it sounded like Joseph had been helping turn Tisdale's Salvation Army headquarters into a hub of humanity. "Now I have keys to the church, the drop-in centre, and the junkyard," he laughed. "It's quite amazing."

His stories were heartening and optimistic, the kind of parables in which a single person really does make a difference. Joseph was so genuinely non-judgmental, so open-minded. It was clear that he considered himself a child of God, but attached himself to no particular faith. "I grew up in both the Roman Catholic and the Greek Orthodox church, but it's all the same God," he had said, shrugging nonchalantly. I raised my eyebrows at his casual certainty regarding religions. "Oh yeah," he assured me. "The churches are all portals to the same thing, girl." And then he laughed: "We're all riding into the same sunset."

And so it was, Joseph said, that when he first arrived in Tisdale, he went on a Friday to the Catholic church, to ask for some palm fronds to use at the Salvation Army church for upcoming Palm Sunday services. "I knew the Catholic church had palms, because I go there often in the afternoon to pray," he'd explained. "It's very serene with the sunlight beaming through the stained glass windows."

Joseph was told that the priest was at the high school that day, conducting the funeral for a local young man, Ryan Smith (not his real name), who had been tragically, horribly killed while working abroad.

And as Joseph said that, I had gotten instant goosebumps. I knew of Ryan; he was the son of my parents' friends. The story of his death was devastating, impossible to forget. But I said nothing, and Joseph had continued.

"So I got back in my truck, and was just sitting there saying a prayer for this young man – whoever he was, I'd never met him myself – when the sweetgrass hanging from my rearview mirror started to swing. And I felt it was someone trying to contact me," he said, concern registering on his face. "I called out the names of my brothers and sisters, mom and dad, my children . . . no, it wasn't anyone in my family. And I called out the names of some close friends . . . no, it wasn't anyone I knew." Joseph shook his head.

That Sunday, he said, after Mass at the Salvation Army, he'd gone home. "And as I lay down on the bed to pray, a vision came to me. In it, I was kneeling and praying at the back of the Salvation Army church when a hand tapped me on the shoulder. I turned and there was this young man standing there. He apologized for interrupting me, but asked if I could help him. I asked him his name, to which he replied, 'Ryan Smith'."

At this disclosure, I had pointedly stared over at my unusual passenger – was he serious? Yes indeed he was; his face was open and honest as he went on.

"I asked Ryan which church he went to, and he told me the Roman Catholic Church down the street. I told him, 'Yeah, I know that one,' and then I asked him what I could help him with. He asked me whether he was dead or not."

Again I'd looked over at Joseph – was he making this up? But his face had been grave, there was a little sadness in his features as he'd been recounting this.

He'd continued softly. "So I said to him, 'Well, as soon as I'm done praying we'll go and see.' I turned towards the front of the church to make the sign of the cross and as I did, I noticed that there was no front of the church or altar remaining. Just huge pillars that went on forever and as high . . .," said Joseph, conveying these structural anomalies with his hands, and then turning to me. "Well, I couldn't even *see* the tops. There were angels in these hues of colour, playing music. They were the softest colours my eyes have ever lain on. It was mesmerizing. But I turned with Ryan and walked out of the Salvation Army church."

By then, I'd been fighting back tears. I didn't want to interrupt the story, but I needed some details filled in. "Joseph," I interjected softly, "what did Ryan look like?"

Joseph was completely candid. "He had short hair, he was tall, handsome, about 23 or 24 I'd say – just a well-built, handsome man," he said. That did fit his description alright. Joseph's expression had then changed to careful contemplation. "He was uncertain, though," he said quietly. "He seemed bewildered almost, about where he was . . . something didn't sit right with him."

Watching the road, I had blinked hard to clear the sudden moisture in my eyes while Joseph resumed narrating his vision.

"So we walked out of the Salvation Army church, and the sky was like today, but as we walked down the street, I noticed to the north that the pillars and the heavenly view were still there. When we went inside the Roman Catholic church, the front of that church and the altar were exactly the same as the Salvation Army, and there was this huge staircase that went up into the clouds too far to see," said Joseph. And here he'd stated that, in his vision, someone carrying a wooden box was coming down the stairs to greet them.

Occasionally when something scares me or excites me, one of my ears will instantly plug up. It had happened right then. I did some exaggerated yawning to open up the passage again – I didn't want to miss a word of this softspoken revelation – and then I'd asked what this 'someone' coming down the stairs looked like.

"He was like a priest or a monk, he was in a black robe. He had dark, shorter hair, his skin had no tarnishes of age at all, he was just really well kept and very beautiful," Joseph said. "He put the wooden box in my hands. I looked in it, there were notebooks and a picture frame with writing in it. I asked him about the box you know, like, 'What should I do with this? Doesn't Ryan have brothers or sisters that should have this?' He told me, 'Yes, but you will know what to do with the box.'"

Joseph shrugged, like he hadn't really understood what that meant, but then he continued with his vision. "Then I said to him, 'You know I actually came here to see if Ryan had passed on or not, and his reply was, 'Oh yes, he's coming with us.'"

Incredulous, I had stared over at this long-haired, bohemian prophet as he casually chronicled the afterlife.

"Then as they walked up the stairs together, Ryan turned and asked me if I could tell his parents and his sisters that he loved them, because he never had time to tell them. He asked me to please pass that on to his family, and to let them know that he's okay. And I agreed that I would do that."

More hard blinking on my part, while Joseph had carried on.

The next day, said Joseph, he phoned Ryan's parents in Tisdale, introduced himself, and told them he'd had a vision of their son that he wanted to share with them. The three of them met the following afternoon at the Catholic church, where he relayed his dream and Ryan's message to the couple. It was when Joseph mentioned the box that Ryan's mother broke down and wept. She and her husband had just come from picking that wooden box up from the school, it was still in their car. The box was full of mementos from Ryan's funeral – notebooks, and a framed memorial tribute.

I had been overwhelmed, stunned by Joseph's story. Especially because I happened to be familiar with this particular family (which Joseph had not known); I could verify that the details of this incredible account were true.

After that story we were silent for a spell. Approaching Saskatoon, there was a fluffy white bank of cumulus clouds with dazzling rays of sun shooting down through sporadic openings onto the rippling fields below. We'd marveled at the effect, and then Joseph said he'd never forget how beautiful heaven was in his vision.

"The colours are different to the eye – they're brighter but softer. It's like a full moon sky with the sun rising and the sun setting at the same time."

Once we'd arrived in the city, Joseph gave me directions to the house where he was staying. It was only a few blocks from my place. He got out of my truck, thanked me sincerely for the ride, and told me to keep the CD. I, still slightly dazed, thanked him for the gift. At the last minute, he suggested we exchange phone numbers. I recited my phone number; he wrote it down, then asked what my last name was. I said "Moore," and he suddenly looked stricken.

"I was supposed to meet you back in 1997," he said with utmost seriousness. "I wonder how I missed you . . . maybe I took a wrong road at some point." With the moment once again in sharp focus, I had asked him what he meant. He got back into the truck to tell the story; it would take a little time.

It so happened that in 1997, Joseph's daughter's friend had invited Joseph and his family to come to her family's Baptist church one evening, to see a special guest. "The Baptist church has always amazed me, because of the energy and the intensity," added Joseph. "Anyway, that night they had brought in a prophet named Dave Redcliff from the States, and lots of different denominations came out to see him because he's highly acclaimed. This man looked out over the audience and he gave different people messages. He pointed to me and he said, 'That man is a giver, and we should give to *him*, because he's been brought to us by God.' And suddenly all these people start crowding around me and my family, and they're all stuffing money into my pockets!" Joseph laughed, wide-eyed.

"It made me feel a little uncomfortable – you know, these people were strangers and they're giving me all this cash! So my family and I got up to make our way out – like politely, *but it was time to go!* And then the prophet called out to me, he said, 'You will meet a family of Moores, and you will give to them.'"

Here Joseph had turned to me, and stated that he'd thought that was particularly interesting because he'd written a song two months prior to that, called "Peace, Love and Harmony." The chorus was: *"Give a little more to the Moores next door, to restore their faith in this world once more."*

Then he'd cued up the first track of the CD, increased the volume, and stated: "I wrote this song for you." With that, he had gotten out of the truck and waved good-bye. I felt a little stunned – *Who on earth was this amazing man?* I kept wondering – as I'd driven home, listening to this song that instantly became one of my all-time favourites.

* * *

Now, a year later, I am 20 minutes on gravel roads past the village of Love. I make the final turn depicted on Gunsmoke's map, and idle up the narrow, sandy path to the cabin. This is God's country: aspen parkland where poplars and jackpine commingle harmoniously, while wild blueberries and fleshy mushrooms thrive below them on the mossy forest floor. In front of a long, low log cabin, I see a parked truck with its hood up, and there's Joseph leaning over the engine. He pulls his head out and smiles as he sees me drive up. He's staying out here for a few weeks as a guest of his friend Bud, while he builds a hangar for Bud's airplane. Joseph has two helpers with him: Ron is a young Tisdale man, and Brian is one of the guitarists in Joseph's band.

Over the next 24 hours, I watch Joseph move gracefully through different roles. I see him as a foreman, a mentor, a mechanic, a host, a musician, a cook, an environmentalist, and a friend. Throughout it all, Joseph is reverent, enthusiastic, and full of allegories about life and God. While chopping wood and building a campfire, his anecdotes roll out. While shopping for camp groceries at the store in nearby Whitefox, his stories keep flowing. While calmly preparing supper for six over an open fire he explores the meaning in life's everyday events.

He creates a constant collage with words, a patchwork quilt threading together all the swatches of his life experience. Layers of characters, events, lessons learned, revelations and blessings; the multi-faceted fabrics of his life. Textiles tenderly sewn together, in worship and in wonder. Joseph, I see, is continually creating his coat of many colours.

This parkland area is prime hunting ground for wild blueberries and the highly prized chanterelle mushroom, so that first afternoon we go gathering. Joseph shows me where to search out the golden chanterelles hiding in patches of lichen, and how to cut them off carefully – just above the ground – leaving their mycelium root network intact. These gourmet mushrooms are coveted in the finest kitchens around the world, but we won't be selling ours to the mushroom buyers waiting in trucks along the roadside; these ones are for our dinner. As I pick, I am aware that this is also prime habitat for black bears, but with Joseph's zeal for storytelling, no bear will be suddenly surprised by our presence. We meander through the woods, our eyes scanning several yards in front of our feet, and I ask him to tell me more about his journey of becoming a healer.

"I gained more interest for healing after I got hurt, and through the experience of other therapists and practitioners working on me," he explains, bending down to finger through some lichen. "The compassion, the understanding, the feeling that's required, my mother has shown me all that and she mentored me, absolutely. But one of *her* teachers was Peter Grabba at Manitou Beach, and Peter was such a wonderful man. He was kind and gentle and humble. Anyway, one summer Mom was cooking at Camp Easter Seal, which is at Manitou, and she got hurt at work. She called me and said, 'Joe, you've got to come help me, I'm hurt and there's nobody else that can run this kitchen.' There were about 160 people in camp, and my back still had severe problems at that time, so I said, 'Mom, that's not just flipping a burger . . . that's lifting big boxes and bags of potatoes – I just can't do it.' She said, 'Joe, we just need someone to organize everything,' so I said, 'Okay,' and I ended up finishing off the rest of that season at Camp Easter Seal."

He stands up and delicately places a handful of chanterelles in the pail. "But before I went to camp, she took me to see Peter Grabba and in five minutes – *five minutes!* – he found my problem, which no doctors had been able to figure out in all those years. I had heard a 'snap' in the accident, and I told Peter that. He showed my mom that this rib was out," he says, now lightly gesturing with his paring knife as a pointer, "and it was crossed over in the middle of the back, touching the nerve. So Peter leaned on my shoulders and it snapped louder than what I'd heard in the car accident. Immediately, it felt like water was running off my back because the swelling was going down so quickly. It was still all swollen even though I'd had cortisone, but Peter said, 'No, you leave those cortisone drugs alone. This is damaged and it'll just take time to heal.'"

Joseph motions to show me a patch of blueberries, and we hasten over to start picking those sweet purple pearls. The first few dozen make 'ting' sounds as they lightly hit the bottom of the tin bucket. "The reality about healing is that you must be able to rest," says Joseph, "because healing comes when you're sleeping. So you must put the body in almost like a spiritual cast, so to speak, and then just watch the body. I did that for about seven years. In summer I lay in dirt for days," he says, laughing. "Just lay there in the dirt between the rows of potatoes in my garden. The garden is so therapeutic. And prayer is most important. Prayer is stronger than anything in the world."

We each empty our cupped hands of blueberries into the bucket. "So how often do you pray?" I ask him.

"I pray continuously," he says. "I thank God for everything. *'Place me where you need me today, God.'* That's my prayer every morning."

Straightening up to stand again, Joseph looks at me. "But healing is a process," he explains. "It's like writing music. Someone will ask me, 'How long did it take you to write that song?'" He laughs with his answer: "Well . . . 41 years! It took 15 minutes with pen and paper, but it took 41 years to bring all the elements together, to experience what's behind it. So I mean, everything went into me becoming a practitioner. I had to get hurt first to understand what it's like to not be healthy. I had to not have money – because I couldn't work for the first time in my life – and it taught me that you can't judge people for things like that because you don't know where they've been. They may have just lost their child, they may have lost their home, you don't know. Love is the most important thing to be able to give. Unconditional love."

Gingerly we step through the forest, watching for patches of lichen with a telltale silvery-ochre mushroom head peeking through. Joseph tells me he now does his own form of body work on people in need, people who come his way. He doesn't advertise or put the word out, but if someone in pain ends up on his doorstep, he figures he is meant to help them. He tells me about an internationally-known speaker named Don Bartlette, who was recently in Tisdale to give a talk during Addictions Awareness Week. Don had many life hurdles including serious physical birth defects as well as abandonment issues from his childhood – followed by years of adversity and addictions – and his motivational story revolves around overcoming these to become the happy and successful adult he is today. He'd flown in from the States for this presentation and was in a lot of pain from the long flight, so Joseph offered to massage him. During the massage, Joseph says he came across a knot in Don's back that he sensed was the physical manifestation of an emotional injury. He said he kept working on this gnarly old knot and encouraged Don to let those emotions go. Joseph says he was right; on Joseph's table that day, Don was able to release the torment of a childhood trauma until the knot was gone. Afterwards, he told Joseph that in the 36 years of weekly therapeutic massages he's had in cities around the world, no treatment had ever come close to accomplishing what Joseph's had.

"Your hands are always guided if you have prayer." Joseph smiles at me. "And I always pray before I touch anyone."

By now, we each have an ice cream pail of chanterelles, and we've got a quarter-bucket of blueberries to boot. We figure it's about 4 o'clock by now; looking up, Joseph comments on the dark rain clouds that have formed overhead. Time to get back to camp and make some supper. Stepping over logs and following animal trails, we make our way through what is now (it seems to me), an infinite tangle of trees. We're aiming a little east of the shadowed sun, which had been directly overhead two hours earlier when we started out.

There's a surreal, almost foreboding quality to this darkening forest labyrinth, and I recall aloud the story of a little girl who got lost in the woods near Tisdale some years back, and died. In this instant I feel such empathy for her and her family. Hers would have been such a frightening and lonely death . . . .

"I've been in the forest and almost been lost, too," says Joseph. "That feeling inside is fear, I guess. You don't know where to turn." He takes deliberate steps in a certain direction and I parallel him. Now getting metaphorical, he says, "And that's when someone comes up, saying, 'Here, try this!' It could be drugs, it could be gambling, it could be anything that's a quick fix – and it's pretty appealing."

"Yeah, that's often the case," I say. "It's when you're weak that you might get sucked into something dangerous. However," I look over at him, "it's also when you're vulnerable that evangelizers and proselytizers might come up, saying, 'Here, try God!'"

"Yeah, it's true," Joseph says, thoughtfully. "Both come at you at the same time." He stops and focuses his eyes on me. "But if you *knew* everything would always be all right, would you be lost anymore?"

I smile broadly at his confidence, at his optimism. Looking around, I spot the green truck camouflaged in the trees and, I admit, I'm relieved. We reach the vehicle just as the rain starts pouring down. Driving on gravel roads through a breathtakingly loud thunderstorm, Joseph is still talking: "People say there are too many choices in life, it's too complicated. Well, if they allowed God to work through them and make their choices, if they asked, 'What's your wish God?', then their decisions, their choices are nil – which actually allows them to enjoy the simplicity of life in this complex world."

Moments after we arrive back at camp, Brian and Ron come shambling up the lane, soaked from getting caught in the flash rainstorm while working at the building site. But the storm quickly moves on; the late afternoon sun is once more shining brightly, and within minutes all is dry again.

Everyone's hungry, so Joseph gets a fire going. He carefully brushes off the chanterelles, cuts them up and fries them in butter over the grill. We four savour the lightly smoked, rich and earthy fungi, then Joseph is up and busy creating supper. He's cookin' up a lot of grub; the rest of the band is coming out to camp later tonight to deliver a new starter for Joseph's truck, and he doesn't know if they'll have eaten. By the time their car comes softly rolling up the sand drive, there are chicken breasts smothered in wild mushroom sauce, new potatoes in butter, a colourful salad full of garden vegetables, and a whole pile of beef burgers sizzling on the grill.

It's interesting to watch these young men interact within their group, their band. There is a palpable excitement and energy around them; this is intensified by the message Joseph received yesterday that a record producer in California has been asking about their band. The four of them certainly *look* like rock stars – long hair, leather jackets and bell-bottom jeans abound – yet they are thoughtful and polite. And they are clearly very admiring of Joseph.

Over dinner I sit with the guitarist, Jay, at the small, wooden table on the cabin porch. It's dark now, with the only light coming from the crackling campfire several feet off from the deck, and the firmament of sparkling stars above us. I ask Jay to tell me more about Joseph. He shakes his head, saying, "The man is phenomenal, he's like no one else I've ever met."

To illustrate, he tells me a story. One summer day a couple years back, Jay says, he and Joseph spent the afternoon at the river. Joseph had lain on the bank, dozing peacefully, while Jay stood for a while in the fast-flowing current. Then Jay dove under. When he surfaced, Jay says, he realized he'd had his expensive sunglasses on the top of his head. Now they were gone. He started yelling and swearing in frustration; he'd *never* find them in this churning water. Joseph woke up, saw the situation, and called out to Jay to move back ten feet. Jay warily made his way back a few steps in the torrent. Joseph then called to him to move three feet to the right. Jay did. "Your glasses are right there!" he hollered out to Jay. "Just feel around for them with your toes!" And right away, Jay says, he found them. When I ask Joseph about the story later, he says that, in that moment, he could clearly see the glasses lying on the riverbed – as if there was no water on top of them.

That night there's lots of laughter, partying, and jamming with guitars. Amidst it there's also lots of swearing – not surprising among musicians, tradesmen . . . guys. Joseph himself says 'the f word' fairly liberally, but one thing he doesn't tolerate is the Lord's name being said in vain. "God created all this beauty around us," he says, "and all this bounty. We should be grateful, not disrespectful." And everyone in the J.T. Styles band obviously is.

By 10 p.m., the three band members are leaving to drive back to town; each of them has to work in the morning. "Blessings on your journey," I hear Joseph say to them at their car, and then I catch a "God bless" in return. Soon after, Joseph and his two apprentices make their beds out of assorted living room couches, and graciously insist I take the private master bedroom.

The next morning, over coffee on the cabin porch, I ask Joseph if his bandmates were believers in God before they met him, or if Joseph had turned them on to Him. He was thoughtful before answering: "I think they see the good things happening to me, the things happening around me . . . they see the state of grace that I get to live in, and I think that's what turned them on. They see how it works." He laughs with those gleaming white teeth. "Because it really works!

"Like I always tell people, if you want something, don't ask me," he waves his hand, dismissively. "But if you *need* something, just ask me for what you need and I can get it for you." He chuckles. "Just recently, this lady moved into town from Alberta, she was a single mother, and I said, 'Is there anything you need?' She said she needed two dressers and two beds for her kids. I said, 'Okay, I'll get you the dressers and beds.' The phone rang not even three minutes later, and it's Bill Wilson from across the alley and he says, 'Joseph, do you need two beds and two dressers because I need to get rid of them.' So I called this lady and said, 'Okay, you're getting your stuff!' and she was in tears, crying. She couldn't believe it." He shakes his head, smiling, and moves the steaming coffee percolator off to the side of the grill to stay warm.

"But I mean, I live in a beautiful community in Tisdale. There's a light there, it's beautiful. People that have come to share my dinner table are everyone from professors, prostitutes from the street, drug dealers, gamblers, robbers – to priests, and children . . . there's all different kinds, different conversations. But hey," Joseph says lifting his arms out in illustration, "God is everywhere."

I can hear Brian and Ron stirring inside the cabin; soon, they'll come shuffling outside, blinking and yawning, to have some breakfast before they go building all day. Joseph is looking pensively out into the trees.

"People have to wake up," he stresses. "You can *see* the energy off the grass, the trees, the flowers, the children, the animals. If you miss that, you're blind. I don't care how well the doctor says you can see, you're still blind."

Joseph swallows the last of his coffee, then shakes his cup at the ground to dislodge the layer of brown sludge at the bottom. He gets up and starts brushing off the grill, readying the cooking surface for the eggs, sausages and chanterelles he'll soon be frying.

I look around at the energy coming off the natural world. The poplar leaves are so green they're vibrating, and the still warm air is humming with the thrum of insect life. "Joseph," I ask him, "what do you think we're here for? Are we supposed to learn something while we're living?"

He refills our coffee mugs. "I'd say that giving is what it's all about. You get so much in return by just giving. Being blessed by someone smiling at you, it's paradise." He breaks into his big grin. "As I travel through life," he says, "I've learned that I am here to enjoy the world as much as I possibly can, max right out on the fun and enjoy the beautiful things that God's given everywhere around me, and just absorb it all. It's one heck of a ride, and I'm glad to be here," he says, now lifting his coffee cup in a 'Cheers!' salute. "And WOOHOO!" he hoots, clinking his mug to mine. We laugh.

After breakfast, I packed up and said good-bye to Joseph, to his two young apprentices, and to that wonderful place in the woods. I left there with a full belly, a bucket full of chanterelles and a bagful of wild blueberries.

I also left there with a renewed gratitude towards that earth energy that sustains us, the wild and gentle energy of the natural world. Mother Nature had fed us lavishly, sheltered us peacefully, and entertained us stunningly over the past two days. The energy in that thunderstorm, the energy from those stars, the energy off that fire, the energy in those mushrooms – it was all indisputable. Scientifically measurable in megawatts and BTUs and caloric values.

Moreso, I left there with a new appreciation of our human energy, our personal essence. Our soul. There is still no good science to capture that most intrinsic feature of a human being; there is still no measure of the soul. There are some theories. I've heard that at the moment of death, the body suddenly weighs 21 grams less, and this has made some question whether that is the weight of the soul. Many esteemed visionaries have claimed to have seen souls.

For myself, I think the soul is manifested in that hopeful, trusting energy of the heart which allows strangers to become kindred friends. I think it's the compassionate energy that responds to others in need, can help them find their way out of the woods. I think it's an intuitive and infinite energy that can show a deceased brother the staircase home.

On my way back to the main highway, I passed through the hamlet of Love again and was struck that it was no coincidence *this* was the place where I had found Joseph Hnatiw. *"Give a little more to the Moores next door, to restore their faith in this world once more,"* I thought.

A huge, happy grin was my expression as I turned up Track 1 of his CD, and headed home on the # 55.

STARGAZING

"We are stardust, we are golden (we are billion-year-old carbon); and we've got to get ourselves back to the garden."

From "Woodstock," Joni Mitchell

I t is a blind date of sorts. We have never met, we have never spoken; I didn't even give her a description of myself when we arranged, via computer, to have coffee at this Saskatoon bistro.

Several months previously, I had emailed her my name and birthdate and requested that she perform a spiritual journey – or personal life reading – for me. Days later, she had responded with four solid pages of writing. Details about my spirit guides, my past lives, my health, my life theme. Her insight and her accuracy had given me goosebumps. I wanted to meet her.

Of her, I know only that she is elderly, and that she does not want our conversation to be recorded on tape. But I can jot down notes. Also, I know that she keeps a fairly low profile and would rather that I don't publicize her name. Stepping into the crowded, bustling café, I stand alongside several others waiting for seats to come open. I start to scan around at the blur of faces when, from the far side of the room, she identifies me and waves me over. As I approach her table, I feel as though I know her.

"Hello!" I beam at her. I am suddenly light and clean and pure, a marked change from the grogginess I was slogging through just moments ago. She stands up to greet me and I see a tall, statuesque woman in a calf-length, aquamarine dress and flat sandals. Her face is smooth, lean and tanned, and not quite congruous with the white hair tied up in a bun. There is an intensity in her features; she has penetrating hazel eyes complimented by a square jaw and strong cheekbones. She appears somewhat abstemious, serious, but I feel her warm welcome.

We sit down at the table together, then order our coffee and tea beverages from a young waiter. She leans forward slightly, and folds her long, sinewy arms over one another on the tabletop. Now studying my face intently, she nods and says she recognizes me by my eyes. Funny: that's how I know her, too. Peering into her eyes gives me the same singular sensation I used to have gazing into my Grandma Moore's eyes, like looking into a mirror. I haven't seen my own eyes reflected back to me so profoundly for many years.

In her time, she tells me, she has conducted hundreds of spiritual journeys for people from all around the world. "Argentina's really big right now." She smiles and shrugs. "I get lots of requests from people there." She says she prefers to know nothing about a person before performing their reading. All she needs from them is their name and birthdate. And although she rarely meets the people, she says she does get a visual image of them.

"Is that how you recognized me when I walked in?" I ask her.

"Well . . .," she begins, then she seems to be assessing me on a larger scale, "there's more." The waiter suddenly appears at our table with coffee and tea; we lean back as he sets everything in front of us. Then he leaves.

Still watching me, she now explains that, in performing these spiritual journeys for others, she has discovered about a dozen others who are – like her, she believes – members of an ancient people that originally came from the stars to populate Earth. According to my four-page reading, I am one of that dozen. I am flabbergasted, maybe even flattered. Although this is a pretty far-out concept to me, I feel completely at ease with her – so I simply accept that this is her belief.

I'm starting to think it is this star connection that compelled her to meet me today. She is now dropping hints it seems, to see if I remember something long past. "One of the Light People," she enunciates, studying me. "Of the stars." I smile back at her appreciatively, but without quite getting it. Still, she *does* seem very familiar to me.

She is considered a Medicine Woman, although she doesn't refer to herself that way. And she is a Pipe Carrier. These traditional roles each bring with them many functions and responsibilities. She has just come off 'the fasting season,' as she calls it. I start right in with excited questions; no need for caution when you're with family.

"So what is the fasting season about? What happens during it?"

She tells me fasting is an aboriginal ritual, in which people abstain from food or water. This spiritual ceremony lasts for four days, she says, and often people will perform four separate fasts, over a span of four years. During the season, she helps set people out on their fast, in a tent or other makeshift structure.

"And you sit there for four days," she explains, "with no distractions. This is how you get your power and your direction. These fasts are very powerful," she intones in a low voice. "Exceedingly powerful."

I look up from my notes to acknowledge the gravity of her statement.

She has done 24 fasts over the many years. "Mine are now done in darkness, for 28 hours," she says, and I gather that this is not the usual method, but rather, her own personal style. "And I know when it's time to do them. My spirits, guides, a voice in my head – I just know when I need it. Without all the everyday distractions, the information can come through."

This information comes to her in dreams and in visions. "The visions are more clearcut and indelible in my mind than the dreams," she says. They are often about others: someone needs to see a doctor; so-and-so must get their hearing checked; someone must perform a certain ceremony. The dreams and visions also provide personal information about relationships. Afterwards, she always relays the information to the people-subjects to use as they want. She believes, absolutely, in the messages.

"When you do this type of work," she explains, "you have to turn yourself over to whatever it is, and trust that you'll be used to your highest power."

I ask, in all politeness, who she turns herself over to.

"When I pray, it's to God and the Creator," she answers, then takes a sip of tea to give me a chance to catch up with my note-taking.

She is not complaining, but being frank when she says that it's a rigorous way to live. "As a Pipe Carrier, there are set routines and protocols that you're taught to follow," she explains. "If you're told to go somewhere, to be someplace, you go. It's fairly onerous, to do the fasting, the ceremony . . . and you have to travel to wherever you're needed. It's not something anybody would *choose* to do," she says firmly. "It's exhausting and it's expensive."

Several times now, she has even been called to work in Third World countries. She's volunteered in Bangladesh with a group called Sleeping Children Around the World, which provides bedkits to the neediest of children in underdeveloped countries. Twice, she's traveled to Sierra Leone as part of a group teaching the widows of war to sew and tailor in order to become self-sufficient. And she is planning to go to Africa for extended periods, to work with victims of AIDS.

"I prefer to work more hands-on," she says. "With widows and children." She herself is a widow who has learned to be self-sufficient. "So this is how I give back in gratitude for all the gifts I have . . . I have so much. I can give away the material things, and live on less."

Indeed, when I had emailed my request for her to do my life reading, she had written back a description of the process, and then addressed the issue of payment most graciously: "I am allowed to charge $50 for this, which goes towards humanitarian work in Third World countries."

I was pleased to be able to contribute to her work abroad, especially after receiving four pages of such perceptively personal material. I now leaf through those pages, look up and implore, "Can you tell me more about my life reading?"

She says she doesn't have much to say about it; she doesn't retain memories after the journey is done. "I do remember that it was a heavy-duty reading, though," she says. "More detail than usual came through."

"And how," I wonder, "do you do a reading?"

"The procedure is that I call on my guides for protection, then go into an altered state where I am met by your totem animal, or animals, who then escort me down and show me what you need to know."

In my case, a gopher and a horse had come forth. The gopher, she had explained, is a dweller in the underworld; it sees under the surface of things. And the horse – well, the horse has always been my favourite creature. To me, it represents freedom, vulnerability, beauty, strength, spirit and wildness. The horse is also my animal symbol in the Chinese zodiac.

"Your totems are always nearby you," she had written, "so you can call upon them when you need a listening ear, support – or you can pray to them. You will probably feel their presence near your right shoulder. They are rather like angels and you, by the way, also have the Archangel Gabriel near you."

Together, these prairie totems had provided data on my present life and the near future, and had put forth some things for me to think about. Two of my 'past lives' were also described in detail. In one, I was a woman standing on the cliffs of a northeastern American state, waiting for the ship to return. I had come over to the new world with other pilgrims, but I missed England – and the overwhelming feeling was one of deep sadness. The ship never came and I succumbed to that winter's illness, without ever finding what I'd hoped to get out of this new life. In the second life-scenario she'd laid out in writing, I was imprisoned in the Tower of London during the 1500s. "This would have been at the time of the King who notoriously banished anyone displeasing him to the tower, often to be beheaded," she wrote. "You were a ladies maid to the Queen at the time and were forced to accompany your lady and serve her in those circumstances in the tower. While in the tower you spent much sad and angry time lamenting your circumstances over which you had no control."

I had no visceral reaction to these centuries-past scenarios, although I thought they were interesting.

"Going back even further," she wrote, "the reason you are doing earth time is that you were brought here from the stars, so to speak. Many souls were sent from the upper dimensions to explore and populate earth – some went back but you were left here which you resented dearly. To this day you still want to go home, you feel a sense of loss and abandonment. This is your life theme – being left and wanting more." Well, I don't deny that I've been affected by loss and abandonment. I just thought it was . . . more *recent*.

"Your colours are yellow, orange and green from the gardens," she wrote. "Surround yourself with them, be it in your clothing or bowls of coloured fruit on your table so you can soak up the colours every time you walk by.

"The stone you need around you is jade – a beautiful green – wear one if possible, be it a pendant or a ring with a setting that allows the stone to touch your skin and pass its healing energy to you. You can also put a piece of jade into your water jug to create a healing elixir as you drink water."

Additional information included my optimal nutrition, which centred on eating more below-ground vegetables in a predominantly vegetarian diet; and using turmeric, as it would apparently benefit me. Also, she outlined some personal health issues and suggested that water was absolutely vital to my well-being. I should live near water, drink more water, be around water. This is very true; the west coast, *specifically* because of all its rain, fog, mist, clouds and ocean remains the place I have always felt most alive.

Along with my request, I had emailed her several questions regarding certain people – some dead – including my maternal grandfather. He was like a gruff Hemingway figure to me: an astute writer and a legendary drinker, who lived somewhat stormily and died prematurely in his 60s. I recall his huge, formidable carpenter's hands; skin cracked, and fingers stained from the filterless cigarettes he rolled himself. When she had asked the guides what he was doing now, the surprising answer was, "He is growing things." And it was then that I remembered the greenhouse he'd built onto the garage, where he tenderly ministered to his beloved tomatoes and peppers. He'd also, I later learned, ran a market garden when he was a younger man. Yes, I *do* believe his soul's purest joy was to grow things. It was life's unrelenting conditions and other people that got in his way.

Hmm. This was an interesting woman who could unearth such revelations. In the reading, she had written: "The loved ones who have passed over are with you in spirit and are always watching over you. They know exactly what is going on with you. You may talk to them or give an intention prior to meditating, letting them know that you wish to consult with them about such-and-such, or that you need advice. They stay with you until they reincarnate back to this plane, and will often come back as someone close to you – like a child or a niece."

One of my email questions was whether our fates are predestined, and this was her reply: "Your soul, your destiny is set, *but* you can bargain and rewrite the slate to a degree. And you aren't going anywhere until your work is done – that is your soul's open-ended commitment. Death, by the way, is simply passing over to another dimension, nothing to be feared – and it always happens when it is meant to, as it has been decided. So we have no need to grieve for someone who passes; it is a happy, glorious time for the soul. It was their time, their choice. Even though someone may have died tragically, it was all planned by their soul."

Now I look up from those written pages as the waiter approaches our table; he refills my coffee cup, then leaves and quickly returns with hot water to fill my companion's teapot. I turn to her again – *Wow, those eyes are uncanny!* – and ask if she is able to see souls.

She answers me candidly, matter-of-factly. "I see souls when they're born, souls when they die. I have been in hospital when people go into Code Blue, and I see their souls floating above their body, leaving."

I'm fascinated. "And what does a soul look like?" I feel a little giddy with the scope of this one.

"The soul looks like . . . nothing that one can describe." She shakes her head. "A glob of light, I guess I'd say; it looks like a glob of light."

"So what happens at the moment of death?" I ask softly.

"My understanding," she says, "is that those who suffer a traumatic death go into limbo, but for the most part, the souls pass into another dimension where they are welcomed, and they rest until they're sent back to do more work."

I am quizzical. "Who sends them back?"

"When a soul is ready to come back to life on Earth, it goes before a Council. Soul says what it will accomplish, the Council says yes or no; if it's yes, the Council specifies who the soul will be with on this next journey, where the person will live, and so on." I get the impression she is contemplating whether or not to continue, and then she does. In carefully chosen words, she says, "I have been honoured to see this Council." It was many years ago, she tells me, in the States, when she was working closely with her mentor – a First Nations shaman.

After some silence, I ask, "Why do souls keep coming back?"

"It's a progression to go forward, up, and to a higher dimension." With all due respect she adds, "That is my understanding of it."

I sip my coffee slowly. Looking once again into her profoundly familial eyes, a memory is sparked. "Oh! Can you tell me more about the Star People?"

"There are Native American legends about our ancient ancestors having been visitors from the stars. My understanding is that these beings were brought to this planet to populate at the same time, but separate from, the Cave People. There were the two facets," she states. "But the Star People were very enlightened, and – as we've been reincarnated from our roots – we still carry with us that enlightenment and the healing powers."

"Why did you recognize me by my eyes?" I prompt her.

"Star People have some common traits," she explains. "They have compelling eyes – usually hazel, green or grey – and they are often big-boned in stature." Interestingly, many were an unexpected child, a 'Star Seed' who allegedly wanted to get down here quickly. (Up to now,

I'd simply chalked that up to my parents being young – and it being the freelovin' '60s!) Star People also, apparently, have a lower than normal body temperature (I've taken thyroid supplements for this, in fact); experience flying dreams (I do regularly); have low blood pressure (surprisingly, yes); and have a rare blood type (less than six per cent of the population shares my blood type). Many have also had an intense spiritual or metaphysical experience, like seeing a ghost.

"So do you believe that you and I are actually related?" I ask, now captivated by this crazy concept.

"Yes, we're all related and we're just finding each other right now, in this lifetime," she states, purposefully. "Right now is a very intense time, there is lots of change, chaos . . . it's a powerful time with high energy coming through. There's an urgency for us to find each other, because the earth is in such a state. As events quicken and we're needed, we'll be called."

"To do what?" I'm a little alarmed.

Referencing the work of Brad Steiger – a paranormal researcher and author of more than 140 books – she tells me that Star People supposedly provide information and an elevated spiritual frequency to planets when a new time-cycle is about to begin. As their level of awareness increases, so does their need to help others, and ultimately to return to their natural state of being – a spark of soul-light. She also assures me that we all do, eventually, return to the stars.

"Whew!" This is getting downright surreal. "So when . . .," I search for words to work with, "is this new time-cycle going to begin, do you think?"

"Many think it will be around the year 2012, the end of the Mayan calendar. We have six years to complete this light-work for the new world."

"And will the earth actually *end* then?" It seems unreal to be having this conversation while around us, I catch snippets of chatter from other tables; one couple discussing what colour to paint their living room, another woman telling her friend about her child's birthday party last weekend.

"My understanding is that, after this time, there will be a New Order where everyone is equal," she states. "There will be no distinction between the races or the genders – no *isms*. What will be left is just one people. There will be unity and love on this planet, like what we had in the star world."

Well I must admit, that does sound quite utopian.

In the meantime, she says, life on this planet is about living consciously and respecting nature and listening to the signs. "For myself, I need to retreat more and more to the land," she explains. "Trees talk, animals talk – that's where I get my signs."

"And what should I be doing . . . do you think?" I ask, tentatively.

She sums up her advice for me: "It's just a matter of believing and trusting that you're always in the exact place you're supposed to be, meeting the people you're supposed to be meeting. There are no mistakes."

I grin at her then. Certainly, meeting *her* has been a fascinating eye-opener for me. After packing up my notes, I thank her for this amazing two hours of conversation, and for the spiritual journey she did for me. We stand and briefly hug one another.

"See you . . .," I start to say, but am unsure how to finish the sentence. "Next time." She confirms the same with a nod. Speculating about just when – and where – that may be, I wander spacily out of the café.

My feet on the ground, my head in the stars.

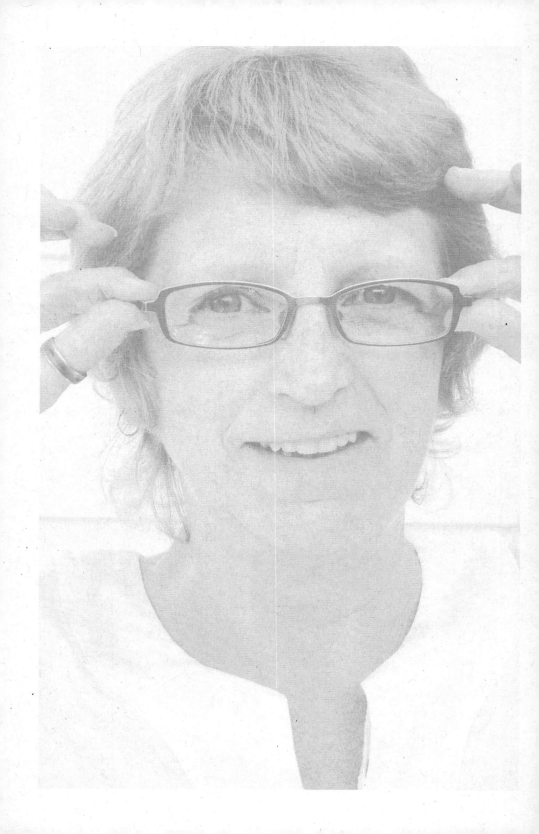

THE MEDIUM IS THE MESSAGE

Necromancy: Divination by communication with the dead

Perhaps the stars were in some kind of kooky alignment that day: Certainly the weather was most erratic on my three-and-a-half-hour drive northeast of Saskatoon, to the town of Hudson Bay. During a sudden deluge of rain, the wipers squeegeed at top speed, barely maintaining a bleary view. Just as suddenly, the downpour stopped and out came the sun with such an immediate and relentless ferocity that the instant humidity gave me a headful of frizz, and wrinkled cotton clothes.

East of Tisdale, the road was fringed with dense boreal forest, and there the lines delineating the two-lane highway became noticeably bright and new. It was on that stretch I saw a bizarre sight: a gopher lying in the middle of the road, dead, with a fresh yellow stripe painted right over top of him. At first I laughed in surprise – it seemed almost comical – but then I soberly wished the creature's soul a peaceful journey. A beacon in yellow he was; and I appreciated that even in death he was helping illuminate the way.

I was on my way to see a psychic medium, a woman who is apparently able to pass along messages from the dead. Her website had briefed me on mediumship: "I'm a conduit for Spirit messages to be transferred to loved ones seeking acknowledgment from loved ones," she wrote. "In grief we want the assurance we're loved and remembered by the one who has crossed over to the other side. We want the comfort of knowing they're well and doing fine, knowing we still love and think of them."

I'd never visited a medium before, and I was curious whether she'd be able to get my number, to connect with anyone I knew. There was an obvious someone – my dad. But it had been 15 years since he died; I wondered if maybe there was a statute of limitations for these things.

As I approached the town, there was a large, folksy sign that read, "Welcome to Hudson Bay, Moose Capital of the World!" and several cartoonish moose heads leaned in from the edges, making goofy faces. I smiled, remembering the plexiglass sign I hand-painted one Christmas, depicting a moose tilting back a beer. I made it for my dad; his nickname was Moose. And he liked beer.

Two intersections and two turns later, I parked in front of the street address on my sheet of directions. Feeling rumpled and disheveled, I walked haltingly up to a bungalow so immaculate it could have been right out of *House and Garden*; the pristine lawn and flowers were perfect enough to look fake. I stopped to smooth out my clothes when, behind me, my name was called. Turning around, I saw across the road a rambling caragana hedge with a gate in the middle, and a woman standing at it waving; behind her was an ageing, two-storey beige and brown house. She unlatched the metal grille and two exuberant dogs came bouncing out – a joyous border collie and a terrier puppy who, clearly, had been waiting to see me her whole life. I then realized I'd written down the wrong address – *How odd!* – but I'd definitely found the right place now. Somewhat relieved, I crossed the street and introduced myself to Pat Hollier.

In her early 50s, she was a tall, slim woman with a red shag hairdo and warm, brown eyes. Her relaxed demeanour was instantly calming. I followed her into the house where we took our sandals off, and then I trailed her into the kitchen. Pat opened the back door and put the border collie out in the yard, saying, "He'll bug us too much." This left us with that maniacal puppy attacking my bare toes, wrestling with my shoes by the front door, and hopping up with tear-inducing nose bonks whenever I bent down to pet her.

Pat's home was comfortable and welcoming, a visual reflection of her personality. Lots of natural pine on the walls and ceiling, a large rectangular dining table that suggested coffee and conversation, and a radio on the kitchen counter that kept up a steady stream of familiar "Oldie Goldie" tunes. All the music I grew up with. She handed me a saucer and steaming coffee cup filled with a sweet mocha beverage, then we sat down at the table across from each other.

There was a liberating lightness and mirth about Pat, as though she had managed to sidestep the bigger burdens that weigh so many of us down. It soon seemed to me she *knew* something; some ancient secret, or life parable. And this knowledge, this insight, freed her to enjoy the journey without worrying about the destination. As we talked, it became clear that nothing was off-limits; Pat was open and responsive to each comment, each moment.

I asked her how she came to be a psychic medium, and she told me she "grew up in a family open to the mysticism of spiritualism." She and her sister were raised by their paternal grandmother who, she added, was a very intuitive woman. "Oh, you couldn't get anything by her," Pat rolled her eyes with affectionate drama. "She knew *everything*." That intuition came easily to Pat, too. "I remember having dreams of things that were going to happen, and then they would," she shrugged. In Grade 8 she was given a pack of tarot cards, and she soon developed her own technique with them. "When I first started reading tarot, I would sit on the floor with my sister and lay the cards all out," she began. "And I thought they were such magical things, because they could talk to you," she said, in awe. "They *told* you things. It wasn't until much later that I realized it wasn't the cards," she said, laughing.

As an adult, Pat went on to become a provincially renowned clairvoyant medium. She was featured in a Global Television production called *The Messengers,* and for ten years did a call-in psychic reading show on Regina's CKRM radio. All told, she'd been making a living as a psychic medium for some 20 years with stints in Arizona, Mexico, Alaska, and the Northwest Territories. Although she didn't advertise, she had an extensive clientele, and performed readings over the phone or in person.

"So," I wondered, "are your readings over the phone as accurate as the readings you do in person?"

Pat nodded. "Oh yeah. Not a problem. I usually shut my eyes and I just listen really hard, and I don't allow myself to think. Because I think Spirit comes between thoughts."

I asked her how often a deceased loved one comes through when she's with a client. She told me she is able to convey messages from beyond in about 90 percent of her readings.

"When spirits come to me in a session, it's because I'm open and receptive to their energies," she explained. "I see and hear them with my heart. It has no bearing on my conscious thought process. I simply allow love's eternal energies to flow freely through me and I say what I'm told." She laughed, almost self-consciously, at the grandeur of that statement.

"Papa was a rolling stone," the Temptations serenaded us in staccato harmony. *"Wherever he laid his hat was his home — and when he died . . . all he left us was alo-o-o-one."* I took a sip of mocha and savoured the song.

"Pat," I ventured, "how do the messages come to you? Are they in words? Or images?"

"Messages come to me in a thought that is not pre-conceived," she stated. "I say it before I even hear it, there is no forethought. It's just instinct."

"And what might the messages be?" I asked her. "I mean, how do they help people?"

Pat nodded before answering to show me she thought that was an important question. "I like to do mediumship for the simple fact that we're comforted by knowing we're still connected." Her voice was smooth, her tone was frank. "When a mother has lost her child and she's grieving deep inside, and she is having a very difficult time in coping and understanding, I can make that connection with her child who's crossed over – and assure her that he's okay, that he's there. I don't just say, 'Oh by the way, your son's over there, he's fine.' I can give her validation, and say, 'Your son's over there and he's saying remember this particular incident, or this particular thing?' And she'll go, 'Oh, yeah!' Because there has to be more, something specific to get confirmation that this is who I've contacted, so the mother can know for sure that it's her child, and she can have comfort in that." Pat sipped from her cup then replaced it on the saucer.

Softly, she continued. "So if I can give this mother a message that will help her feel better, to get past it, then I know I've done good. If I can give a reading to somebody that takes them from a place of despair to a place of hope and promise, then I've done a good job. That's how I see it, that's what it's for."

She now asked if I'd mind if she smoked. I shook my head, saying, "No problem." I'd quit smoking a couple years ago, but I still enjoyed the smell of roasting tobacco now and then. Reminded me of my dad.

Pat's readings also pertained to a person's present life. First, she said, she would give details on where the person had been, to make sure she was 'getting' them properly. Once that was satisfactorily established, she would help them figure out where they're going.

"The people that are hardest to read are people that have issues, and they don't want to deal with these issues and they're blocked," she said. "In some cases, I will suggest that they see a counselor – sometimes people need that kind of professional help if it's really deep emotional stuff. I don't see that as a weakness; I see it as being strong enough to deal with their issues, to become better people."

We'd finished our coffees, and she asked if I'd like another one. "Yes, please!" I answered, enthusiastically. While she got up to make them, the radio took centre stage. A male Motown group crooned a soft melody: *"People get ready, there's a train a-coming; you don't need no baggage, you just get on board."* It was about dying, I supposed – I'd never really listened to the lyrics before. Pat placed our cups on the table, and sat back down.

"Can you see death when you do a reading?" I asked her. "Can you tell if someone is going to die soon . . . or of what?"

"Yup," she answered matter-of-factly. "In fact, my brother-in-law, I saw his death. I saw my grandmother die. I do, I see people die." She took a sip of mocha. "And I can *feel* death," she said, setting her cup back down. "I know what it feels like."

"What does it feel like?" I asked quietly.

She sighed. "Almost like a panic attack, but not quite, when you know it's coming . . . ."

"Is it like a sneeze?" I asked.

"Yes!" Her face lit up.

"Like going into a sneeze but you don't sneeze?"

"Yes! And then when death hits, it's just calm."

I nodded in understanding, and a little relief. I had been with my dad when he died. I'd always worried that his peculiar facial expression may have signified pain. Or fear.

"I can see clearly now, the rain is gone." Oh, Johnny Nash, I remembered his name from an old K-Tel album. *"I can see all obstacles in my way."* Such a reassuring song. I'd forgotten it. *"Gone are the dark clouds that had me blind . . . it's gonna be a bright, bright, sunshiny day."*

"Pat, how do you get answers in your own daily life, how do you know when you're on the right path?"

"I look for things constantly," she asserted. "Signs and validation. I listen to the radio, what song it is. I look for animals – if I see a crow or a raven stop and stare at me and make a little noise, then that's confirmation. But it has to be significant," she stated, as the telephone now shrilly announced a caller. She got up and walked over to look at the call display. "It's my husband Chris, I'll just take this," she said, then quickly summed up her previous line of thought. "So, I'm always looking for something. And I'm always aware." Pat answered the phone and was soon chatting cheerily about tonight's dinner plans.

Yes, I thought, *I watch for the signs, too.* I'm often astonished by the serendipities in everyday life. Musing about a friend from a different city, a whole different time in my life, can spark some form of contact from that person within days. Conversation topics – even specific words – will be mirrored by background music. Idle imaginings or curious wonderings end up being the subject of that evening's TV or radio program. There are patterns and there are portents, although I recognize them mostly in hindsight . . . I gazed down at my yellow pad of paper, then flashed on the yellow-striped gopher.

Pat hung up the phone and breezily sat back down. Again, I got the impression that this woman had some rare knowledge – like the secret to the Chinese folktale, in which the wise old man moves mountains with the most simple and overlooked logic. She had some crucial understanding which enabled her to live with such peace and confidence. The more I talked with her, the more I felt she was a woman freed from the existential worries of life.

I was curious about something. "Pat, is there such a thing as bad spirits?" I asked. "Like, have you ever encountered negative entities?"

"All the spirits that I've ever communicated with – whether the people had committed suicide, shot themselves, hung themselves, shot somebody else and then shot themselves," she listed, almost impersonally – "whatever those people did, they are not like that in spirit at all." She shook her head in emphasis. "They're *full*. They're full of love and compassion and caring. They're love. That's all they are, they're just a pure energy of love," she said. "And they want the very best for us."

I recalled a session Pat had written about on her website, a session in which a certain man came for a reading. "And to his surprise," she wrote, "a young spirit came by to say 'thank you' to him. The man was reduced to grief-stricken tears at his own memory: it had been a bright sunny day and as he returned home from work his mind was occupied with the day's business. He turned down his back alley and was blinded by the setting sun. The sun's bright light hit the windshield in such a way it hampered his vision. Unknown to him, a young boy, against his parents' wishes, was on his bike and, fearful of being caught, raced down the alley and zipped across heading towards his back driveway." The man did not see the bike before his car struck it, killing the boy. And this man had never been able to forgive himself for ending that child's life.

"The boy told him forgiveness wasn't necessary, that there was nothing to forgive," recorded Pat. "He wanted to thank the man for aiding him on his journey, as he was an angel ready to return home. The incident will never be forgotten by this man, and even though he couldn't understand, he knew he had to accept that he was without blame."

Pat told me that through the years she's been doing spirit-work, she's had some realizations in life. "The biggest one is that our thoughts do control the quality of our existence. Our thoughts stem from innermost feelings we have about ourselves. And as Spirit says, we don't need to forgive anyone – not even ourselves – because forgiveness is not necessary. What's done is finished. Even the negative moments in our lives enable us to grow and to improve as human beings. After all," she said, smiling, "we've always been Spirit; there's only a brief interlude where we learn how to be human."

This prompted a question I was keen to have answered. "So Pat, what are we supposed to learn, as humans?"

"The goal while we're living is to learn how to be a human being," she stated. "To just be. We're not here to be Buddha," she added. "That would be boring!" Her eyes sparkled playfully. "I think it's just to learn how to be human, and to accept others for being human."

"Think of your fellow man, lend him a helping hand . . . ." We both listened to the radio for a moment. Pat lit a cigarette. *"Put a little love in your heart."*

"I have a philosophy," she said, exhaling smoke away from me, "that we are all connected. We all interlock, we all fit into one another. Each and every one of us. So if this person can become better, then I can become better, then you can become better. And if this person falls, we're going to go down too, so we'd best pick that person up. Put on some rose-coloured glasses, choose to see things in a better perspective, bring them back up."

We smiled broadly at each other. Then Pat butted out her cigarette; it was time for my reading. She got up from the table, washed her hands at the kitchen sink, and led me into her office. She was obviously excited about her shiny new leap in technology: a laptop computer. There was no need for me to take notes; the attached microphone would record the entire reading, which she would then put on a CD for me. We sat at a small table, across from one another.

"Okay, first off, I need your hands," she said, and I placed them on the table. "I don't consider myself a palm-reader," she explained, "but I do feel the energies that come off the hand. And sometimes I see images in the palm," she added noncommittally. "Or words, too." Holding my right hand with her left one – which was noticeably warm – she then glanced casually into my upturned palms.

"You've been doing a lot of internalizing," she said assuredly. "You're like a bear in hibernation, you're on this inner journey of self-discovery."

She pointed to some lines in my left palm. "And you're meant to be a writer – you've got this awesome writer's fork right here, so this is definitely where you need to be!" I grinned at her appreciatively.

"You have a man with you, in spirit," she announced. "A father figure. Has your dad passed on?" she asked.

"Yes," I said, and swallowed. Up until now, I'd not mentioned a word about him.

"Okay, because he's right there with you," Pat nodded emphatically. "Oh, I *like* this man," she smiled, now looking over my right shoulder. "He's a great guy, he's lots of fun." I chuckled softly, remembering his laidback attitude, his sense of humour.

"He died suddenly," she stated, her face now serious.

"Yes," I said.

She was watching over my shoulder, as if listening to someone speak, and then she broke out in laughter. "He says he's *very* glad you dumped that guy!" Instantly I felt my face get hot. I had promised my dad just before he died that I would break up with my boyfriend at the time, a guy who had completely obliterated any chance of my father liking him. But that was a very select bit of information, which no one knew.

"He says he's very proud of you, of who you've become," she continued. "He's proud of your accomplishments." Through warm, blurring tears, I worked to focus on Pat's every facial expression. "He wants you to remember something, though," she said, thoughtfully. "He wants you to keep in mind that the glass is not half-empty, it is half-full."

I sighed in agreement. That is a very good reminder for me; one of my life lessons, really. She looked back at my palm.

"Do you have a two-storey house?" she asked.

"Yes," I said.

"And do you have a big staircase that has a wall on one side, and then it's open with a banister on the other side?"

I nodded. "Yes."

"Okay," she continued, "and the staircase is wood, but there's some carpet, too."

"Yes."

"And there's a landing," she said, now looking up, into my eyes.

"Yes."

"Well, that's where this spirit likes to be, he has shown me that image," she declared. "Any idea why he likes that spot?"

I thought for a moment. "Not really . . . although his sister – my aunt – gave me a framed birchbark-biting done by an elderly Cree woman, and it hangs right there. I would have to say," I continued, thinking aloud, "that it's one of my favourite spaces in the house, too." I thought of how, every morning as I descended those stairs to start the day, I felt like Scarlett O'Hara sweeping down the staircase of Tara. *(Dear reader: right now, I am at the top of those same stairs, in my office typing that paragraph when the phone rings. A male voice politely asks for 'Wayne.' I tell the caller he must have the wrong number, and he sounds surprised: "Really?! This isn't Wayne's number?" I assure him it isn't, then hang up the phone. I turn back to this story, and am struck by the coincidence: my dad's name was Wayne.)*

"Anyway," Pat went on, looking into my palms, "your health looks good, you're very strong. And you're a healer," she announced with renewed vigour. In response to my muted surprise, she attested, "You've got a lot of healing in here," then added, "and that could be through communication. Because when other people are telling you their stories, they're healing themselves. And when you're telling your stories, you're healing yourself. And when you're going through stuff, you are a person who has to articulate it, you have to speak it aloud, and then you finally find the answer somewhere in that. So . . .," and she seemed to lose her train of thought.

"Okay, your dad's interrupting me," she said, chuckling. "He thinks it's very important that you realize more about death, about the moment you're dying." My heart started pounding; I'd been troubled by his dying moment for the past 15 years.

"He says that nobody ever dies alone. That there's always somebody who comes to get you, and eases you through that transition. And that you don't suffer, your body does not hurt. You're always out of your body when there's pain and suffering. He says that it is so beautiful, so peaceful, so exciting, that any unhappy things you had inside – like disappointment, or hurt, or failings – just disappear, like they never existed at all. And then you know that everything is fine, that everyone is fine. You go across ever so gently, and reunite with everyone. But he says it's not an ending, it's a beginning and you go home. So you're not afraid, because you've been there before – before you come here, that's where you are – and when you leave here that's where you return," she said, now peering at me.

"Coming *here* is actually more scary!" She laughed lightly, while reassuring me with her big, warm eyes. "But he says all those little things in life that we get trapped up in, that we get caught up in, really aren't important. At the end, what was important was that you were creating a landscape or a picture and you don't know what it's going to look like until you're finished. You have to go in the direction that's right for you, and not worry about anybody else." Pat nodded earnestly, to show she agreed with this message she was transmitting from my father.

Then she was more thoughtful. "Your dad is a gentle soul, and I think in life he was a gentle soul. I get lots of writing around him as well."

"Yes," I confirmed. "He wrote poetry."

Pat was quiet, looking beyond my shoulder. "He's definitely there, he watches over you," she said, distracted. "And also around him is another woman, I think it's his mom. I also get a child, a boy. But he doesn't say anything."

I smiled through tears. Most certainly, my dad would be keeping company with his wonderful mother, and with his brother who died in infancy.

"Your dad talks to me about a time when you were young and you were sick with spots, I don't know if it was measles or chicken-pox. And he sat with you, and he teased you. He wants you to remember those times. He doesn't want his death remembered, he wants the joys that you shared remembered."

Pat cocked her head a little. "As for your mom and him, I don't get him strong around her – not at all – were they divorced or something?"

"Yes," I said, "when I was young."

"Yeah, they weren't on the same page," Pat said, shaking her head. "Not even *close*," she stressed dramatically, and together we laughed because it was so very true. And it was also okay.

Pat consciously shifted herself on her chair. Now looking again at my palm, she said, "I see you have a significant friend named Kailey . . . Kalli," and she stammered a little with the pronunciation of this unusual name.

"Yes," I said, "Kahlee, the Root Woman. I just talked to her this morning." Pat nodded vigorously, and looked back into my hand.

"And do you have a sister who lives away?" she wondered.

"Yes, I have a stepsister who lives in Vancouver." I didn't add that we were once very close – she's one of the people who most shaped who I am, she's one of my favourite people in the world – but in recent years we'd lost some connection. I found this new distance between us upsetting. Pat proceeded to tell me that my sister was having a hard time right now, that she was at a real crux in her life and had no energy to give to others.

"Yes!" I jumped in. "That's exactly what I felt the last couple times we saw one another." It had worried me, in fact, but Pat assured me my sister would get through this and our special relationship would one day be on track again.

"All in due course," she said to me. "Everything is fine between you two."

This was timely and helpful. I'd been debating whether to try and talk with my sister about our detachment or let things naturally unfold. Now I knew to bide my time.

On Pat's website, she writes that although she does not know God's plan, "I do know in my heart all love is universal and it is only the mind preventing us from recognizing it or understanding what love truly is. As Spirit has said to me, love is a free energy flowing through each and everyone. When it's controlled, it's no longer love."

* * *

I write this now from memory. It turns out that the gleaming new laptop computer captured two CDs full of loud, crackly static; the entire two-hour psychic reading is gone. Furthermore (and I now know this is not just an excuse for failing to turn in homework), the few notes I took were actually eaten by my dog. After my initial disappointment, there was frustration, even a little panic. But eventually I had to laugh because this was all just the capriciousness and the unpredictability of life.

Thanks to a wonderful, whimsical clairvoyant medium out in small-town Saskatchewan, I can see clearly now that the glass is indeed half-full. Because Pat's messages from my dad were relevant and poignant to me, I take solace in knowing that even in death, he helps illuminate my way. And this belief – that our spirit, our essence, does not die – is granting me a more fluid, wholesome perspective on the natural cycle of life and death.

During my drive home from Hudson Bay that afternoon, the radio was playing in the background when on came my dad's all-time favourite tune; a song by Harry Chapin called "All My Life's a Circle."

"It seems like I've been here before, I can't remember when;
but I have this funny feeling that we'll all be together again.
No straight lines make up my life, and all my roads have bends;
there's no clear-cut beginnings and so far no dead-ends."

I'd heard that song hundreds of times before, but this time it had new significance for me. This time I got the message, loud and clear.

Endnotes

Reading Between the Lines:

Page 16 – Nathaniel Altman, *The Little Giant Encyclopedia of Palmistry* (New York: Sterling Publishing Co. Inc., 1999): p. 11.

Page 17 – Michael Scotts, *De Philsiognomia,* 1477. This was a book on the physiognomy of the human anatomy which included a chapter detailing all facets of the hands. Physiognomy is a pseudo-science exploring how a person's appearance and bodily characteristics reflect their character and personality.

Page 19 – George Catlin was the first and probably most famous painter of Native North Americans. In the early 1800s, he produced several hundred portraits of people from some 50 different tribes.

Page 20 – Adam McLeod, *Dreamhealer - His name is Adam* (Canada: DreamHealer.com, 2003): p. 18-19, 46.

The Wax Pourer:

Page 29 – Rena Jeanne Hanchuk, *The Word and Wax: A Medical Folk Ritual Among Ukrainians in Alberta* (Toronto: CIUS Press, 1999): Introduction, p. 2.

Page 33 – Ibid., p. 1.

Page 38 – Ibid.

Page 40 – Ibid.

Ben E. Diction:

Page 44 – Nathaniel Altman, *The Little Giant Encyclopedia of Palmistry* (New York: Sterling Publishing Co. Inc., 1999): p. 414.

Root Woman:

Page 52 – Lewis Carroll, *Alice's Adventures in Wonderland* (New York: Avenel Books, 1865): p. 68. Three-inch-high Alice said to a hookah-smoking caterpillar sitting atop a mushroom that she'd like to be a little larger. The caterpillar told her: "One side will make you grow taller, and the other side will make you grow shorter." He was referring to the mushroom.

Page 53 – *Harold and Maude* is a 1971 film directed by Hal Ashby. It features a young Bud Cort (Harold) and an elderly Ruth Gordon (Maude). The fantastic soundtrack is by Cat Stevens. Although the film was never a commercial success, it has garnered a huge cult following over the years.

Page 54 – Rita MacNeil is a world-renowned Canadian singer from Cape Breton.

Page 55 – Thornton Burgess was an American conservationist and children's author who wrote more than 150 books about much-beloved characters such as Billy Mink, Sammy Jay, Reddy Fox, and Grandfather Frog.

Page 56 – Kahlee Keane and Dave Howarth, *The Standing People: Field Guide of Medicinal Plants for the Prairie Provinces* (Saskatoon: Save Our Species, 2003): p. 104.

Page 57 – Lewis Carroll, *Alice's Adventures in Wonderland* (New York: Avenel Books, 1865): p. 3. It was the White Rabbit that led Alice down the rabbit-hole.

Page 58 – Ibid., p. 15. "Curiouser and curiouser!" Alice cried, as she grew in height to nine feet.

Page 58 – Kahlee Keane and Dave Howarth, *The Standing People: Field Guide of Medicinal Plants for the Prairie Provinces* (Saskatoon: Save Our Species, 2003): p. 104.

Page 58 – Ibid., p. 216.

Page 59 – http://gaian.ca

Page 60 – Lewis Carroll, *Alice's Adventures in Wonderland* (New York: Avenel Books, 1865): p. 9. When Alice first fell down the rabbit-hole, she came across a little bottle with a paper label and the words "DRINK ME" on it. The contents had a "mixed flavour of cherry-tart, custard, pine-apple, roast turkey, toffy, and hot buttered toast . . ." After drinking it down, Alice shrunk to ten inches high.

Also see http://rootwoman.com

Of Hartmann Grids and Pyramids:

Page 64 – *De re metallica* – "On the Nature of Metals (Minerals)" – is a book published in 1556. For 250 years, it was the authoritative text on the art of mining, refining, and smelting metals. Agricola describes methods of prospecting for underground minerals, including dowsing. The book includes an illustration of a German dowser in action. http://en.wikipedia.org/wiki/De_re_metallica

Page 65 – http://www.angelfire.com/nj/healing/dowsing.html

Page 65 – Brian Leigh Molyneaux, *The Sacred Earth*: Little Brown & Co. (P), 1995. http://meta-religion.com/Spiritualism/Wicca/dragons_guardians_earth.htm

Page 66 – "A number of ley lines criss-cross in the centre of Stonehenge. Ley lines are a natural magnetic phenomena that cross the countryside. Ancient monuments often are sited at the intersection of such ley lines. Even in Saxon times, non pagan churches were built on a ley line. If you see a church aligned say north-south instead of the traditional east-west, the odds are that a ley line runs straight down the aisle." http://www.londontoolkit.com/whattodo/stonehenge_history.htm

Page 66 – Dr. Joseph Mercola, http://articles.mercola.com/sites/articles/archive/2000/08/13/geopathic-stress.aspx

Page 66 – "The human brain in a healthy state has also been shown to oscillate at 7.83 Hertz." http://www.active-water.com/en/schumann_frequency.html

Page 67 – Brendan Murphy, http://www.positiveenergy.ie/GS/WhatIsIt.htm

Page 67 – Ulla Schmid, http://www.healingcancernaturally.com/geopathic-stress-and-cancer.html

Page 68 – Ibid.

Page 68 – David R. Cowan, http://www.leyman.demon.co.uk/14%20Unhealthy%20Earth%20Energies,%20The%20Hartmann%20Net%20and%20Curry%20Gri.html

Page 68 – Dr. Joseph Mercola, http://articles.mercola.com/sites/articles/archive/2000/08/13/geopathic-stress.aspx

Page 68 – Rolf Gordon, http://www.rolfgordon.co.uk/

Page 70 – Beata Van Berkom, http://www.circlessoundandcreation.com

Page 71 - http://www.bltresearch.com/history.php

Page 71 – Freddy Silva, http://www.cropcirclesecrets.org/education.html

Page 71 - http://www.amcollege.edu/earthacupuncture.htm

Page 72 - http://www.gizapyramid.com/featured_research_of_the_week.htm

Page 76 – Joey Korn, http://www.dowsers.com/page4.html

Luminous Mysteries:

Page 80-83 – Carmen Humphrey, http://www.carmenhumphrey.org/testimony_3.html

Page 84-85 – Francesca Iosca-Pagnin, *Reflections 'Npink* (Saskatoon: 2004): p. 59-61, 69.

Page 85 – Ibid., p. 63-64, 69-72, 99.

Page 86 – Ibid., p. 106, 113, 197-198.

The Boxer:

Page 99 – Visit the Saskatchewan Sports Hall of Fame and Museum at www.sshfm.com

Page 105 – http://www.evalu8.org/staticpage?page=review&siteid=1836

Into the Mystic:

Page 117 – http://en.wikipedia.org/wiki/Fort_San,_Saskatchewan

Page 122 – http://www.taigarescue.org/en//index.php?sub=2&cat=2

Page 133 – http://www.catholic.org/prayers/prayer.php?p=683

Page 134 – http://www.shapeshifter.name/

Page 136 – http://www.absoluteastronomy.com/topics/Altered_state_of_consciousness#encyclopedia

Wisdom of the Sages:

Page 140 – http://www.vedicvidyainstitute.com/palmistry.html

Page 141 – http://en.wikipedia.org/wiki/Karma_in_Hinduism

The Chrysalis:

Page 153 – http://www.candacepert.com/

Page 153 – http://www.med.unc.edu/wellness/main/links/cellular%20memory.htm

Joseph and His Coat of Many Colours:

Page 178 – http://en.wikipedia.org/wiki/Duncan_MacDougall_(doctor)

Stargazing:

Page 188 – http://www.v-j-enterprises.com/jufobook.html
Page 189 – http://www.crystalinks.com/starseeds.html
Page 189 – http://www.adishakti.org/mayan_end_times_
prophecy_12-21-2012.htm

The Medium is the Message:

Page 199 – http://phoenixconsulting.piczo.com/voicesfrom
beyond?cr=6&linkvar=000044

About the Author

Jacqueline Moore is a Saskatchewan freelance writer. Over the years, she has been a dessert baker, a tree planter, a features reporter, a racehorse groom/stablehand, a desktop publisher, an environmental educator, and a couple dozen other things. She studied French at l'Université de Montreal, and the Humanities at UBC in Vancouver before eventually attaining a diploma in journalism. Having always been fascinated with others' life experiences, it was her years spent as a journalist that gave Jacqueline the language to write their stories.

Since writing this book, Jacqueline is learning a new language: equine. Suddenly finding herself with two horses, she's pretty much in the immersion program. Jacqueline and her husband Scott live in an old house in Saskatoon with a big goofy dog, and an outrageously demanding elderly cat.

Jacqueline is an alumna of the Saskatchewan School of the Arts (Fort San, 1982) and the Sage Hill Writing Experience. Throughout the years, she's had the good fortune to study creative writing with Guy Vanderhaeghe, David Carpenter, J. Jill Robinson, Steven Ross Smith, Sharon Butala, Sue Goyette and Phil Hall. She's begun work on her next collection of true stories; this one about crazy, tragic, and hilarious life.